D0016100

More titles by Dr. Henry Cloud

The Secret Things of God
The Law of Happiness

DR. HENRY CLOUD

NEVER GO BACK

10 things
you'll never
do again

HOWARD BOOKS
A DIVISION OF SIMON & SCHUSTER, INC.
New York   Nashville   London   Toronto   Sydney   New Delhi

Howard Books
A Division of Simon & Schuster, Inc.
1230 Avenue of the Americas
New York, NY 10020

First Howard Books hardcover edition June 2014

HOWARD and colophon are trademarks of Simon & Schuster, Inc.

For information about special discounts for bulk purchases, please contact Simon & Schuster Special Sales at 1-866-506-1949 or business@simonandschuster.com.

The Simon & Schuster Speakers Bureau can bring authors to your live event. For more information or to book an event, contact the Simon & Schuster Speakers Bureau at 1-866-248-3049 or visit our website at www.simonspeakers.com.

Interior design by Julie Schroeder
Jacket design by Brand Navigation, LLC

Manufactured in the United States of America

10 9 8 7 6 5 4 3 2 1

Library of Congress Cataloging-in-Publication Data

Cloud, Henry.
  Never go back / Dr. Henry Cloud.
    pages   cm
  1. Regret.   2. Becoming (Philosophy)   I. Title.   II. Title.
  BF575.R33C46 2014
  158—dc23   2013048296

ISBN 978-1-4391-8054-9
ISBN 978-1-4516-6932-9 (ebook)

*This book is dedicated
to my clients, friends, and mentors
who have shared their lives and their wisdom with me.
I would be making a lot more U-turns were it not for you.*

ACKNOWLEDGMENTS

A book is a journey, with many guides and helps along the way. I have been guided and helped in this journey by many, and here are a few I would like to thank for this book:

- To my clients . . . thank you for sharing your lives and work with me. I truly appreciate you.

- To my agents, Jan Miller and Shannon Marven. You make publishing a pleasure and a shared mission. I feel bad for those who do not have you and still try to write books! How hard that must be!

- To my editor, Philis Boultinghouse. You are a true gift and pleasure to work with. I wish all editors were more like you!

- To my assistant, Lexi: Thank you for making all the pieces work and for keeping me going with your life-giving attitude and spirit.

- To my family: Thank you for the fun and joy that fuels me when I am trying to get through the writing season!

- To my friends: Thank you for bringing life to me.

- To God: Thank you for your life and wisdom.

CONTENTS

THE NINETEEN-FOOT
SPINNING JESUS

I was excited about my upcoming meeting with the television executive. He was working with one of the major networks on a project he wanted me to consider. He was familiar with some of my work and some associates had told him to contact me. We had a great telephone conversation about how I would approach the topic he wanted to address, and he had really connected with what we had discussed. Until . . .

I walked in and the maître d' escorted me to his table.

"Hi, I'm Henry. Good to meet you face-to-face," I said.

"Hi," he said. But his demeanor was not as exuberant as it had been on the phone just a few days before. After we ordered our food, he did not waste any time and jumped right in to let me know why.

"So . . ." he began. "I Googled you."

"Yeah, and what did you find?" I asked.

"When I typed in your name, it was as if a *nineteen-foot spinning Jesus was over your head.*"

"Uh . . . *what?*" I asked. I had not ever seen Jesus hovering over me, so I was a bit surprised and confused.

"A lot of the stuff you have written and talked about is so *religious*," he said. "When we talked, you seemed pretty normal, so I was kind of shocked. I mean, you *are* a real doctor, right? But in one clip I could not tell if you were a psychologist or a preacher. You were talking about God and Jesus and a whole bunch of religious stuff. So, what gives?"

I laughed so hard I spewed out my coffee.

"I totally get it," I said. "The 'spinning Jesus' and 'you seemed normal' make me laugh, but it is a real issue sometimes."

"How so?" he asked.

"Well, exactly what you said," I went on. "My professional life is serious to me and very scientifically based. I spend a lot of time deep in the research of clinical, relational, and performance issues. So, yes, I am a 'real doctor,' as you said. And most of my work is in very mainstream, secular settings, like this network or CNN or Fox, or corporations or leadership events where the topic has nothing to do with faith or spirituality. What I talk about fits in because when we are discussing what causes depression or a relationship breakdown or a CEO's destructive behavior, I work from very real principles and research-based science. That is why you connected with what we discussed on the phone. Just 'normal' psychologist stuff, as you say.

"At the same time, although I am not particularly 'religious,' to use your term, I *am* a person of faith. I have come to believe that all of science and research strongly validate what my faith tradition teaches. So sometimes I have an opportunity to speak, write, and work in contexts where I talk about faith too. So I am not surprised that you ran across some of that material. Don't get scared," I said, still a bit amused at it all.

"Well, you said your expression of faith sometimes causes issues. What might those be?" he asked.

"The look on your face when I walked in!" I said. "I have seen that look before."

"What look?" he asked.

"You summed it up when you said, 'I thought you were normal, and now I find out you are one of those religious types.'

"Because I also write about faith and how it affects our lives, sometimes people associate me with weirdos they have met from religious groups, and I have to work to convince them that real faith is not weird at all. So sometimes I have to overcome an extra step—guilt by association with the kooks. It's just that I see and experience great compatibility with spiritual wisdom and scientific knowledge, and for me, they validate each other over and over. I see no conflict."

"Okay, that makes sense . . . I think," he said. "You didn't sound crazy when we talked, but I just wondered. It scared me."

"Well, I am a bit crazy in my own ways, as my family and friends will tell you, but nothing that requires institutionalization," I said. "Just garden-variety dysfunction."

He laughed, relaxed a bit, and we moved on to talk about the project he wanted to do.

So, what does that encounter have to do with this book?

A lot.

This television executive was afraid that I might be too "religious" for him. And in my experience, many people have this same fear about matters of faith. Anything that sounds too spiritual makes people wary, and they immediately turn off. I do not want that to happen with this book, so I wanted to start with a few words about where I am coming from.

The foundation of this book is twofold: (1) Successful people have certain realizations, or awakenings, that change the course of their lives forever in a positive way. These realizations are essential to a good life and are both scientifically and spiritually backed. You'll see that there are obvious correlations between science and research and the spiritual teachings of Scripture. (2) Realizing the validity of these principles is only step one; step two is making real change in your life. So I'll share with you some foundational concepts about life change that will help you make those shifts a reality.

Here is a bit of how it comes together for me: I believe that God is the source of all of wisdom, as the designer of life and the universe. He knows how life works and has given us the secrets to this life through the Jewish prophets and Jesus. The Bible prolifically reveals the secrets to life, reflected in the name of the series this book is a part of, "The Secret Things of God." So, in this series I get to share both of my favorite things—the science of life and the life of faith—and how these two relate. In a sense, in this book I get to be "all of me"—both a psychologist and a person of faith.

So, I have three requests of you, my friends:

First, I want you to explore and benefit from the principles in the book that research and experience tell us are true. Use them and see. I hope you find them helpful in your life, relationships, and business.

Second, if you do not come from a faith perspective, please do not let the spiritual language and the quotes from the Bible turn you off. Hang in there with me and keep reading so you can benefit from the science and from the experience of successful people.

Even if at first glance it seems like a spinning Jesus is hovering over my head.

Third, if you have had some bad experiences with people from the faith world or with spiritual language, please reserve judgment and take a fresh look with me. Take the spiritual writings that I share, the Bible verses, at face value; please don't view them through the lenses of the kooks you have known or seen on TV. Believe me, I am with you and have the same negative reaction to those people myself.

But I have learned not to let the crazies ruin faith for me, and I would like for you to engage with me in this book to take a fresh look. Faith and spirituality might be very different in reality than may have been expressed to you in some sad distortions. So if you would, take a real look at the spiritual principles I share. Try to see their great, great wisdom, which I believe shows that Someone truly did design it all and wants us to know him and know more about how life works than we can discover on our own.

God and faith are not weird. My own relationship with the very real, living God and the realization that his ways are true is what saved my life back when I was really suffering. And ever since then, he has sustained me, grown me, and led me into a life I never thought I could have.

My prayer is that this book, in addition to sharing some great life principles, will also give you a fresh look at God, and I thank you for the opportunity to share it.

NEVER GO BACK

I remember the moment like it was yesterday. I was sitting on my patio after I had found out that one of my businesses was in very serious trouble. I had hired someone to run it who, for close to a year, had given me strong and positive reports. I had no reason to think anything was amiss . . . until that morning.

He came into my office and told me that we needed a big infusion of cash to meet upcoming obligations. I was shocked. Everything he had been telling me had put me in the mind-set of expecting a big *payoff* in the near term, not the necessity of a cash infusion—and certainly not one of the size he was asking for. What the heck had happened?

I went into fire-drill mode and uncovered the truth by late afternoon. Suffice it to say, much of what he had been telling me was not true. We were not making money at all; rather, we had been losing money and were in big trouble. And worse, most of the business that he had told me was in the pipeline and secure for the next twelve months was not real. The reports he'd been giving me were more about what he had planned than about reality. Bottom line: The business was in the red and had little revenue set up for the next year. I was devastated.

So that night I went outside on my porch to sit and think and talk to God. That is when it happened. The phone rang, and when I answered it, my heart sank. It was one of my business mentors, a man who had been an immense help to me since I had first begun and who had poured much time and energy into me over several years. He was enormously successful in numerous industries. It seemed that everything he did worked, and he was the last person I wanted to talk to at my moment of failure. How could I tell him how stupid I had been to allow this to happen? He was going to fire me as a student for sure. I did not want to talk to him. Only loyalty and gratitude kept me from saying, "Sorry . . . no one here by that name," and hanging up.

"What's happening?" he asked, just checking in.

"Well . . . a lot. And it's not good," I said.

"What? What's going on?" he asked.

"I have a horrible situation . . ." I began. "I have really, really screwed up." I went from there to tell him the story and the situation I was in because I'd hired the wrong person and hadn't been fully aware of what was going on in my business. I felt so foolish, so naïve . . . and just dumb. It was horrible to have to listen to myself relay it.

When I finished the story, the phone was silent. It was probably only a handful of seconds, but it seemed like an eternity. All I could think was that he was going to fry me for being so stupid. Then he said it:

"Well . . . we've all been there."

"What?" A bit stunned, I thought I'd misheard him. "*We?*" That sounded as if he had done the same thing himself, and that was certainly not possible. Everything he did always seemed to turn out great. What did he mean?

"Been where?" I asked.

"Made that very mistake," he said. "Hired the wrong person or did a deal with the wrong partner, should have seen it coming, and paid dearly for it."

"*You've* done that?" I was having a hard time believing my ears.

"Absolutely," he said. "Anyone who has ever built anything or done anything significant has made that mistake. We've all had to learn that one."

But what he said next was the real zinger:

"But the good thing is that once you learn
*that lesson, you **never go back**.*
You never do it again."

That phrase *never go back* caught my attention, as I knew that I didn't want to repeat what I had done ever again. I didn't want to entrust something important—like my business—to someone unworthy of that trust ever again. My friend had my attention. The phrase "never go back" resonated.

And it is now the subject of this book—*Never Go Back: 10 Things You'll Never Do Again.*

"Never go back." Never return to what didn't work. What does that mean? I came to see that the essence of it is this:

There are certain awakenings that people have
—in life and in business—
that once they have them, they never go back
to the old way of doing things.
And when that happens, they are never the same.
In short, they got it.

That was years ago. From there, I began to be very interested in two things in my work as a clinical psychologist and leadership coach. First, what are key awakenings that successful people go through that forever change how they do things and that propel them to succeed in business, relationships, and life? Identifying these keys could change lives significantly.

And second, once we intellectually understand what we should never do again, how do we actually change? It's one thing to "understand"; it's quite another to live out that understanding. Unfortunately, we humans often repeat the same mistakes over and over again. How do we stop?

In this book, we will look at these two questions:

1. What are some of the key *awakenings* that successful people experience?
2. How do we implement in life what we intellectually understand?

In my experience, both of these are key. In working with people who are highly successful in their personal and business lives, I have found that the answers to these questions are essential to completing the picture. Some people have learned *how* to implement change but cannot see the life-patterns that are holding them back and keeping them from fruitfulness. In this book, we will clearly identify destructive patterns and behaviors that you'll never want to go back to.

Other people understand *what* they need to awaken to, but don't know *how* to translate that understanding into new life-patterns. In this book, I'll show you how.

An "Old, Unpopular, Religious, Negative" Word That Will Change Your Life

When I first got the idea for this book, I wanted to title it *I Repent!* My desire was to revive this old religious term that gets a bad rap. But I kept getting negative reactions to the idea. I'd literally hear things like . . .

"Gross!"

"Too negative."

"Sounds like an old angry preacher with white hair yelling at me. I would never read that book."

"Terrible. Too negative. I would never pick it up."

But then I would explain what the book is about. . . . "It's really cool. It is about certain realizations that successful people have in life, and *once they 'get it,' they never go back to seeing or doing things the old way.* A shift occurs in them that leads to lasting change in key areas of life, such as happiness, relationships, and business. I like to think of it as a kind of 'mental puberty.' In physical puberty your body changes and you go through doorways never to come back. There is a permanent shift in body and mind. The pubescent youth literally *changes.*

> I like to think of it as a kind of "mental puberty."

"The same is true with our psychological, personal, and business growth. When we go through certain doorways of understanding, we never go back to our old way of seeing things," I said. "People who are happy, successful, and have good relationships have gone through certain common awakenings. Once they get it, they are done with the old way and never go back."

"That's a *lot* more interesting than repentance," I would hear. "I'd read *that* book!"

That is why you're now reading the book *Never Go Back!*, formerly known in my mind as *I Repent.* But I do want to give it one more try with you and put a positive spin on an old negative word. "Repentance" truly is your friend, and brain research proves it. More about the research later.

True Repentance—Never Going Back—Means
Understanding Reality

The response I got about an old angry preacher yelling at us pretty much illustrates the problem. People think of "repentance" as having to do with a parent, preacher, nun, or teacher scolding them and saying, "Don't ever do that again!" It is a religious term with a lot of cultural baggage. It feels like a parent or authority figure telling you to stop doing something, and then you feel like you just *have* to do it. That is a problem.

The reason is this: whenever we get our backs up at a message that says we should not do something again, it *shows that we are out of touch with life's realities.* Picture a parent telling a toddler to "repent" from running into the busy street. The toddler just looks at the parent *as if the message or the messenger is the problem,* sets his face in determination, and says, "Just watch me." Dangerous indeed.

Such is the nature of the word "repentance." Repentance is the adult equivalent of stopping at the curb and making sure no cars are coming before you cross the street—especially an adult who has experienced the reality of being hit by a car once before because she didn't look. It is the realization that she does *not* want to do that again. It is *not* going to feel good. It felt really bad last time and it will feel bad again. And the realization of and commitment to that reality are stronger than the need, desire, or impulse to do it; so we are *forever* changed. We are no longer people who run into the street or hire the wrong person when we knew better—losing a lot of money, time, and energy in the process. We have *repented,* or literally "changed our mind and turned away" from that way of doing life. That is what the word actually means. In another word, we experience *growth*. Or *maturity*. Or better yet, *wisdom*.

I would love to see myself and the people I care about and

work with have realizations every day and begin saying, "I repent! I will never do that again!" and mean it. That would indicate that we see the word as the positive force it truly is: a gift from God.

But, human as we are, I won't try to force the word "repent" on you. You can call it something else if you want. What I will try to do is to help you to see the power of "getting it," which means really, really, really changing your mind about some key realities that are keeping you from what you want out of life—personally or professionally—and *turning* from them. Whatever you call it is okay with me. I think "repent" is cool, but "never go back" is okay, too.

So in the first part of this book, we'll explore ten key realizations about behaviors and thought patterns that hold us back and keep us from our goals. When you actually "get" the principles in the first part of the book, and then implement the helps you'll find in the second part, you will never want to go back to your old ways—you will be forever different. You will never again . . .

1. Return to what hasn't worked
2. Do anything that requires you to be someone else
3. Try to change another person
4. Believe that you can please everyone
5. Choose short-term comfort over long-term benefit
6. Trust someone or something flawless
7. Take your eyes off the big picture
8. Neglect to do due diligence

9. Fail to ask why you are where you are
10. Forget that your inner life produces your outer
     success

The above are realizations that successful people live by. And successful people all got where they are the same way. In every area of life, successful people change and grow into success via a predictable path that both experience and research document, and that the Bible describes and commands. They understand the very real consequences of doing things in an unproductive way; they "get it" in a way that transforms them, and they never go back to doing it the old way. The key realizations for success in all areas of life and the pathway to implementing those realizations are what you will learn about in this book.

So if "repent" rubs you the wrong way, then let's turn away from ways that don't work, and "never go back." Let's hop into them.

PART ONE

——— ◆ ———

Never-Go-Back Awakenings

It was good for me to be afflicted so that I might learn your decrees.
—Psalm 119:71, NIV

PRINCIPLE

Never go back to what hasn't worked.

CHAPTER 1

NEVER AGAIN . . .

RETURN TO WHAT HASN'T WORKED

I was on the beach in Hawaii with my daughter Lucy when she was nine, the last day of our vacation. She looked across the sand and noticed that our friend who was traveling with us was crying.

"What's wrong with Laura?" she asked.

"She and her boyfriend Jason had a fight," I said.

"WHATT??????" Lucy exclaimed. "She went back with Jason??"

"Yep," I said.

"NO! Dad, why did she do that?" she asked. "Remember *last* year on our last day of vacation? She was crying when she got off the phone with him then, too? This is the very same thing all over again. Exactly the same. Why did she do that?"

"You'll have to ask her," I said.

"I will," said the young sage. "She cannot go back with him. It will just be the same thing next year. I have to tell her."

I could not believe my ears. I was amazed at the wisdom of a child, so insightful about what was happening. Yet our adult friend was unable to grasp the glaring truth she was living out.

Here she was, one year later, in the same situation, crying the same tears, and still lacking the awareness that next year would hold the very same promise for more pain . . . if she did not see a fundamental reality:

If you go backward, you are going backward.

Laura had been in this relationship for about four years. Her biggest complaint was that Jason took her for granted and did not make her a priority. He was a nice guy, but too self-centered to make a relationship work. Over and over again, he would leave her feeling ignored and unimportant. She had broken up with him several times, missed him, reunited, and nothing had changed. She would break up with him again and then a few months later would run into him and, with the pain gone, begin to enjoy all the good things about him and want to try again.

They would both talk about how they had been foolish to break up with so much good in their relationship, how they really loved each other, and how they truly should be together. "I was wrong to leave. I miss you and want to be with you again," would be their mutual feeling. So they would get back together and do it again.

So what's wrong with that? Everything. But please understand something: I am *not* saying that people should not be allowed to have second, third, or fourth chances. The story of redemption is the greatest story ever told. It's natural, and sometimes good, to try again. When things go bad, especially in relationships, we want to find a way to make them work and to restore love. When business deals go bad, we want to be able to fix them and make them work. When we fail at a dream or career, we want to be able to come back and win. The story of every successful life includes failure, misses, and obstacles that are overcome. Redemption and restoration are good things and God's true desire for us all.

But here is the real truth when it comes to redemption versus going backward: if redemption is to occur, *something must be different*. A second chance is not a repeat of the first chance. A second chance is a moving *forward* to something *new*. There must be something new and different in order to move forward rather than backward. If everything's the same, you are repeating what already has been, and there is no reason to think the outcome will be different.

> A second chance is not a repeat of the first chance.

Laura's plan to get back together with Jason was not because she or Jason had become a different person or grown in some way. She was getting back with Jason because she hoped that their relationship could be different. *Hoping* that we or someone else will change or that a situation will be different is not reality. There must be a real reason to believe and try again.

Had Jason gone through some awakening himself, other than he was "sorry" and wanted her back? Had he gone into therapy? Had he gotten a life coach to teach him how to make a relationship work? Had they gone to counseling together to find out why they had failed and what they needed to do to make it work? Had he followed through on any of that? Had he stopped

his psychological dependency on marijuana that he called "rec-
reational" but that always got in the way of their relationship?

No.

So when Laura went back hoping that it would be different
this time, there was no real reason to hope. As I said in my book
Necessary Endings, hope without realistic
reasons to believe is not hope at all. It is
only a "wish." God gives us a solid way to
tell the difference between a hope and a
wish. It is called "fruit." When a tree gets
healthy, you can see the blossoms and the
fruit that prove it has life in it. When a per-
son or a situation has truly changed and is worthy of our investment, we will be able to see tangible reasons to believe.

> Hope without
> realistic reasons to
> believe is not hope
> at all. It is only a
> "wish."

One of my favorite examples of this truth in the Bible is in
the book of Matthew. John the Baptist is the messenger prepar-
ing everyone for Jesus' arrival. He is at the river baptizing people
who were repenting and asking for forgiveness. Then he notices
that a bunch of known religious hypocrites were taking part. He
calls them a "bunch of snakes" and confronts them:

Brood of vipers! Who warned you to flee from the coming wrath?
Therefore produce fruit consistent with repentance.
—Matthew 3:7–8, HCSB

Said another way: *Sorry is not good enough.* Something has to be
different. True repentance can be seen in the real "fruit," or results,
it produces. The Message Bible puts the above scripture this way:

Do you think a little water on your snakeskins
is going to make any difference?
It's your life that must change, not your skin!

In both translations, the idea is the same: *Something has to be different.* There must be fruit, results, or a real change in life or the situation that gives reason to believe that something will be different this time. So here is the main concept:

If you "go back," make sure you are going forward.

That way you are not going backward just to repeat what has already been. You are truly moving forward because something tangible is different. Someone being "sorry" (ourselves included) is not enough; just missing the good parts of what was is not reason enough to return; going back to assuage the pain—temporarily, mind you—is not enough. Life is meant to be forward moving, not backward. Make sure that if you "go back," you're not going back to the same thing.

In business, we often see this when someone ends a relationship with a boss, a company, an employee, a strategy, a partnership, or even an industry. They move on for a while, only to go back and do it all over again. They rehire the person or go back to work for the same boss or company that they left for good reason or some other redo. For some reason, they think it will be different this time. Yet they find themselves back where they were to start with.

Remember: *There is a reason it did not work. If you are going back, make very, very sure that reason is no longer there*. You need to see more than just a "sorry" or a commitment to make it work "this time." You need to see a real, verifiable change. People do change, and people do learn. Situations change; dynamics that were once present and making something not work can be different now. People build skills, learn new things, develop new capacities, etc. That is what life is about, and all of our lives hopefully are in a direction of getting better, not worse. Just make sure that is the case before you "go back" to anything.

Me, You, or It

If you are considering going back to anything that did not work or that you had a good reason for leaving, look at three categories of possible change, asking these questions:

1. Am *I* different in some way that would make this work?
2. Is the *other person* or persons different in some way that would make this work?
3. Is the *situation* fundamentally different in some way that would make this work?

Am I Different?

Sometimes you are the one who did the leaving and has changed. I see this often in family businesses where an adult child leaves the family business either because of conflict with the parent-boss or a drive to "make it on his own" or because he has simply not grown up in some way. So things don't work out, and he leaves.

Time passes, the adult child works in other places, experiences failures and successes, or gets the "need to be on my own" out of his system. He has grown up, feels less like a child under the parent's control, or whatever. He comes back into the business and is very successful, fulfilled, and happy. But the important thing to note is that the child has truly changed and matured.

If you are that adult child, be honest in examining your reasons for going back: Have you grown up and matured and now feel ready to settle down in a family business or move back to your hometown? Or are you coming back simply because things didn't work out for you and you need a rescue? Hard questions that must be answered.

Sometimes going back can work when expectations have changed or matured and the wish for something different has been given up. I see that sometimes in marriages that are put back together and reconciled. But if the relationship is going to work, something must be different in the expectations of the one who left and is coming back. If you're the one who left and now want to return, look at yourself to see if you have truly changed or are simply coming back because you're lonely or sad. There must be something *different* in you if you want to make something work that didn't work before. Likewise, if you are the one who stayed, before taking back the one who left, ask yourself, "What is different? In me or the other person?"

If you have had problems with addiction or self-centeredness or being overreactive, controlling, or perfectionistic, you must make significant changes for things to be different. If you go through a meaningful awakening or get into real recovery or take a chill pill or mature in relationship skills, then something truly is new. Then, when you go back to your spouse or significant other, you will be going forward not backward. The relationship has a chance of working because *you* are a different person.

The key here is this: if you are going back to a job, person, relationship, town, or whatever, the question to ask is, *Have I changed in some significant way so that what I am going back to is truly what I want and what I am capable of making work?* Not just because I *desire* for it to work, but because I am *different* in a way that will make the relationship or situation different? Is this a going forward or a going backward? In what tangible way has my change proven itself? Where is the "fruit" in my life?

Is the Other Person Different?

In the second instance, the question to ask is, *Is the* other *person or persons different in some way that would make it work?* If we left something because another person's behavior or character was unacceptable—not our own expectations or reactions— how is that person different now and in what tangible way is that fruit being lived out?

For example, if you left someone because of their addiction, do not return just because the person says they are sorry and won't do "that" anymore. Return when sorry has shown fruit, like involvement in a recovery program and a track record of sobriety. Or if it was a character issue, has there been a change in spiritual and personal growth that is showing trustable results?

Just because someone is sorry does not mean they have changed. It may mean they *want* to be different, but you must be able to see tangible fruit to know the change is real. Forgive people freely for the past; but in order to trust them for the future, you need to see tangible changes.

> Forgive people freely for the past; but in order to trust them for the future, you need to see tangible changes.

Is the Situation Different?

In the third instance, there must be some real change in the situation that would make it work. The company has new ownership, the market is different, the leadership has changed, or different people are involved in the situation. Look for tangible evidence of change for the better so that you will be going forward not backward.

I am currently considering doing a business deal with someone I worked with in the past who did not perform well in that particular situation. He had enormous strengths in certain areas and glaring weaknesses in others. Ultimately, his weaknesses caused his company to fail, and I suffered some consequences in his failure. Due to his weaknesses, I did not get all that he had promised in the venture.

So what about now? Why am I considering doing another deal with him? Good question, and one that I have not fully decided upon yet. But I will let you in on my reasoning, applying the principles we are talking about here.

If he were starting another company and raising money for

it and wanted me to invest, I would say absolutely not. No way. He is not a CEO, and I would not invest in something that he would be overseeing or depend on its performance. Been there, done that. Do not want to go back. Love the guy, but am not going to depend on a company he is running.

But, in the current venture, he would not be running anything. He would be performing in a capacity that I have seen him do very, very well in his old company. He has good character and great drive, and is a proven performer in doing the kinds of things I would need in this situation. So the situation *is* different. It is not a "going back" to what was. I am thinking about it.

What I must do is compare his real performance in that area to other candidates who I am considering. Real against real. But when I told a friend of mine that I was thinking about doing business with this guy, my friend looked at me and said, "Are you crazy? Don't you remember the mess he made?"

Great warning. Now I just have to decide if this situation is different enough so that his enormous strengths can be utilized or if I am fooling myself and going back to what I should "never go back" to ever again. If I write a sequel to this book, I'll let you know what happened! But for now, I'm asking myself, *Is this situation different enough so that success is probable?*

Tomorrow, Not Yesterday

When considering going back, think of it this way: next year is next year, not last year. Tomorrow is tomorrow, not yesterday. God has designed life in a way that is forward moving. As time moves forward we grow, develop, and transform into newer, more complete and mature lives. Unless . . . we are stuck. And there is no better way to remain stuck than to repeat what has already been. The last thing you want to do is relive the past all over again. Tomorrow should be new and improved—always!

When a person comes to this realization, it's usually because he has made the same mistake twice or more. He has gone back to some situation or person that he had left behind, thinking and hoping it would be different "this time." But he found, instead, that the old situation simply repeated itself. At some point in the journey, he realizes, "I was here before and I left. Why did I come back to do it again? How is it that I find myself here again?"

That realization, if listened to, can become a great teacher. It is the wake-up call that says, "You knew this was what it was like. Yet you came back. You should have known better than to think it would be different this time." That understanding becomes a prediction when the person finds himself considering a repeat. His memory reminds him: "Remember when you went back before? Where did it get you? It got you right back to what you had left and for good reason. No need to repeat it."

And when it becomes a real awakening, that memory is not just about a specific situation. It becomes a memory that can apply to all situations: *If you left for a reason, you left for a reason. And if that reason is not gone, then you will be right back there again. Don't go backwards.* This new understanding becomes a structure inside our wisdom brain that puts up the caution light and says, "This will not end well." Go for tomorrow, not yesterday. Unless, of course, yesterday was great and you truly want to do it again. Nothing wrong with that at all—if it truly was great. Which brings us to a major reason we return to situations and people that were *not* that great.

Selective Memory

Often, when we want something back that we had rationally decided we didn't want, the "something" we want is not really the "something" we left. It is an idealized version of the thing or person we want—it is not reality.

When my friend would talk about wanting to go back to her boyfriend, she would talk about how she missed the connection they had, his wit, his brains, his creativity, and the fun they had together. *That's* what she wanted back. And then I would say something like, "I do not know the person you are talking about."

"What do you mean?" she would say. "Those things are all true about Jason."

"I know, but when you describe him, you describe him as if those things were the total picture of who he is and what being in a relationship with him is like. In truth, the person you are missing is not the person he was. You're missing the parts of him that don't exist without the other parts. If you are going to miss him, ask yourself if you miss the connection, the wit, the brains, the creativity, the fun, *and* the self-centeredness that would ignore you for days on end, the non-responsiveness, the accusations of your being too needy if you wanted him to show up, the accusations of your being controlling and smothering if you wanted him not to go out most nights with his friends and leave you alone, and the anger. If you are really going to ask yourself if you miss him, *ask yourself about the real him, not a fantasy version of him that doesn't exist.*"

When I would bring those things back to her memory, she would get sane again and would remember the disappointment in the kind of person he really was. She would feel a healthy grief over the loss of an unhealthy relationship, instead of longing for an idealized version of Jason that would cause her to pick up the phone and do it all over again—or believe him when he called and tried to convince her to come back.

If you are planning to go back and yet nothing has changed, make sure you know you are going back to what was and still is, not what you *wish* would be. If it truly is different, fine. But if not, do not make it different in your head.

The Bottom Line

If a nine-year-old can tell you that you should not go back, then the decision is not rocket science. It is a matter of being in touch with reality, looking it squarely in the face. You know what was, so if you do not want what you left, make sure you are going back to something different . . . either in you, the other person or people, or the situation. Otherwise, you are doing the same thing expecting different results. And that is a pattern from which we truly want to repent. We should *never* go back to the same thing expecting different results.

We have different gifts, according to the grace
given to each of us.
—Romans 12:6a, NIV

PRINCIPLE

**Never go back to doing something that requires you
to be somebody else.**

CHAPTER 2

NEVER AGAIN . . .

DO ANYTHING THAT REQUIRES YOU TO BE SOMEONE YOU'RE NOT

When I entered college, life for me was all about playing competitive golf. I was recruited to play at a great golf school, Southern Methodist University, and I was looking forward to the next four years. It was my longtime dream-come-true.

Unfortunately, I suffered a hand injury during my freshman year that hampered my ability to play well, and I struggled for a couple of years before finally having to quit. My dream was lost, and it was a very hard time. So what to do?

When I enrolled, I thought that if I did not pursue a career in golf, I would go to law school. I liked the subject matter, especially business law, and all that I knew about the profession. And I was good in math, so my advisors directed me to select a major that would dovetail well with business law; everyone told me I should choose accounting and finance. It would draw heavily upon my math strengths and prepare me well for that field. Tax law, business law, corporate law, etc., would all be open to me.

In the summer of my sophomore year, I felt I needed to get some practical experience in the financial world, so I went to a bank and applied for a job. I passed all the tests, and they made me a teller at a local branch.

The training was interesting; I learned about how all the daily transactions worked, how to balance the ledger, and how to make the numbers work. So far, so good. I began my stint in the teller's window.

It went well for the first week while I was in training. I had a nice lady supervisor who oversaw my work, and I dealt with customer transactions, deposits, withdrawals, etc. I enjoyed learning all the pieces.

But in the second week, I was on my own in my own booth. Of course, I had to keep tedious, detailed records of everything that went on, so that at the end of the day everything balanced. Gradually, I figured out that I was in trouble. Something about all of that minute, detail-focused work made my brain swim. At times, I would feel as if I were on autopilot, a bit detached from my body. Something about having my head buried in details all day was not me, even though I had a math-inclined brain. But I kept going. Until . . .

One day a lucky customer—probably a nice little old lady in my small town—hit the jackpot. She came to my window to do a transaction, and I gave her the fifty dollars in cash that she wanted to withdraw. The problem was that earlier that day, when I had prepared all of the stacks of cash and coins, I had somehow misplaced or mismarked a stack of fifty-dollar bills as one-dollar bills. So I thought the stack was fifty one-dollar bills, when in reality it was a stack of fifty fifty-dollar bills. When I thought I had given her fifty dollars, I had actually given her twenty-five hundred dollars. She won the lottery, never to come back.

The bank decided that I was not coming back, either—at least not as a teller or anyone who was able to get close to the money. For the rest of the summer, I worked in the stockroom, moving boxes to trucks. So much for my career in high finance. Counting boxes was not exactly mutual funds or investment banking.

But I learned something. While I was good in math and big-picture conceptualizations, such as analyzing balance sheets and profit-and-loss statements, I was not good at keeping track of minutiae. The "detail chip" was not installed in my brain. And the more I had to deal with the details of the numbers, the less I was able to do well. I would unplug and lose horsepower. I would get worse, not better. Now I am sure that some of it was the immaturity and irresponsibility of the nineteen-year-old I was, but it was more than that.

It was just not me.

I began to question my major field of study. The numbers thing, even at a high level, was not looking like a fit. In fact, it was looking like a major misfit.

The more accounting courses I took, the more the same issue emerged. I liked the concepts and the big picture, but the line-by-line accounting work was for someone else. Could I do it? Yes. Could I get the right answer? Yes. Could I keep doing it for a long period of time and sustain it? If I had to, yes, depending on how long is long. But a really long time, like a career?

Absolutely not. I was drying up inside and hating what I was supposed to be loving. It was just "not me."

> I was drying up inside and hating what I was supposed to be loving. It was just "not me."

At the same time, I was beginning my spiritual path and doing a lot of reading in theology, psychology, and philosophy. When I did that, *something came alive in me that did not awaken when I was reading my accounting and finance books*. It felt very different. This "something" had energy and could hold my effort and attention endlessly. In my spiritual community, I was spending more and more time in discussions about life, problems, growth, challenges, personal changes, spiritual growth, and the like. I could not get enough of it.

Finally I faced the music. I had to change my major, and I began to sign up for psychology classes. As I pursued this new subject matter, a whole new world opened up to me. I came alive. It was me, and I knew it. The time flew! I was in a zone.

Getting in the "Flow"

Time really does fly when you are engaged in a "this is me" experience—what researcher Mihaly Csikszentmihalyi has termed as being in the "flow." Sonja Lyubomirsky, in her book *The How of Happiness,* explains that in Csikszentmihalyi's flow "the sense of the duration of time is altered: hours pass by in minutes, and minutes can stretch out to seem like hours. The combination of all these elements causes a sense of deep enjoyment that is so rewarding people feel that expending a great deal of energy is worthwhile simply to be able to feel it."

Flow was way different from my "not me" financial experience—where hours seemed like decades and the sensation of time slowing down was never pleasant—like it can be when you're in the flow.

Oh yeah . . . there was one other difference: performance. When I found what I loved and was more suited for, I actually performed better. That is another aspect of "flow":

Engagement fuels higher performance.

So what does this have to do with "never going back"? Everything. I learned a principle and went through an awakening that now, decades later, I believe in more than I even did then:

*If you have to be someone else
in order to do something,
don't do it.*

Trying to be someone else simply will not work longer than a little while. The real you will come out in various ways, fighting on the outside—actively or passively—or dragging you down from within. Personhood—as God has designed it—is something to be fed, nurtured, matured, grown, and expressed. If it isn't, it ends up expressing itself in negative ways.

When Not "Being Me" Is a Good Thing

I am not saying that we should never do things that are "not me." Sometimes that's actually the responsible thing to do. Like taking a job that is not who you are in order to support your family or to pay for an education or an illness. But notice something about that. Even though you may have to do something that is not fully "you," you do it for a reason that *truly is you*: the love of another person or family or mission, or a decision driven by circumstance. And if you do it for sacrificial reasons, your motivating factor truly *is* you. That can change everything. The key is whether or not your motivating factor is a good one and whether or not you stay in touch with it.

I hate early mornings, but for years as a competitive golfer, I got up before the day began and went to the range for an hour or two to practice. Mornings are "not me," but golf was.

Sticking with God's Design

God has made you a certain way, with certain abilities and inclinations. The Bible refers to these abilities and inclinations as *gifts*. The research world refers to them as *strengths*. What we know from God's word, as well as years of scientific research, is this: *you will do better in work, life, and relationships when you are acting in accord with who you truly are, versus trying to be someone you are not.* Being who you truly are fuels performance, in all realms.

In my early college days, the feeling that I had to be someone other than who I was around church people was one of the things that kept me from serious spiritual pursuits. I always felt like I had to be someone different in order to fit into "religious settings."

When I began to seek God in college, however, he led me to a group of people that I could be myself around. I found that, with them, I could be a person of faith and still be in my own skin. In fact, it was even better than that. In this community of faith, I not only could be myself, I found parts of myself that I never knew existed. In a real sense, I became more of myself than before.

That is what God says should happen to us when we are in a real relationship with him, real relationships with others, and involved in the kind of the work and activities that invests in the real us. As wise King Solomon said:

> *There is nothing better for people*
> *than to be happy and to do good while they live.*
> *That each of them may eat and drink,*
> *and find satisfaction in all their toil*
> *—this is the gift of God.*
> *—Ecclesiastes 3:12–14, NIV*

So before you invest yourself in a person, a relationship, a team, a company, a career, a church, or anything that you will become a "part of" in a meaningful way, ask yourself this question: *Can I do this and still be me?*

Choices That Change Lives

I know a surgeon who did not want to be a doctor but became one because of multi-generational family pressure. What he really loved was music and art. But he got squeezed into the mold of his grandfather and father. He tried to be someone he was not.

Eventually, his "real self" found a way out. He had an IQ of about a million and had great skills, yet somehow he managed to continually make mistakes—like leaving sponges and tools inside of people—until malpractice claims and disgruntled hospitals made the decision for him that he should have made for himself years before: the doctor thing was "not him."

But this is not only true in work. I know a woman who desperately wanted two things: marriage and prestige. Sandy got both when she fell for Ben. The problem was that Ben's personality, culture, family, lifestyle, and society were regimented, formal, image-conscious, and filled with protocol. Being associated with Ben meant being associated with all that came with him.

Sandy did not fit in—not with Ben and not with what came with him. No way. But she had fallen in love with the fantasy of it all and tried to be someone she wasn't *in order to have what she desired.* Ben and his family stifled her, and the social settings she had idealized shackled and constrained her. She found herself resentful, depressed, and smothered. It was not her. But because Ben came with the status she badly wanted, she denied that the relationship interfered with who she truly was. She had the outer trappings she had always dreamed of, but she was miserable and resentful on the inside.

Compare that to Christine, a big-time New York entertainment executive whose life was a whirlwind of power meetings, exciting ventures, and incredible settings and activities. She was not a small-town girl, by any measure. Until she met Luke.

In their relationship, she found something that was even more of who she was than her career, and she gave up her career to follow Luke across the country to a small community. She was not faking it or molding herself into someone she was not. She gave up some things willingly to have something she wanted more. There was no resentment at all.

Life is always about giving up some treasures for others. Christine found new ways to express her drive and creativity in her new setting—while remaining true to who she was. She became more of herself, not less. Unlike the surgeon, she did not experience relationship "malpractice suits." Relationship malpractice suits include breakups, bitterness, a lack of love, and lots of resentment. Christine's was a clean sacrifice.

What I'm *Not* Saying

Before we go on to see more of what God says about being true to ourselves, I want to be clear about what I am not saying.

I'm Not Saying "It's All About Me!"

First, I am not saying go back to the "me generation" of the seventies. Horrible idea. The trend of that era was to be so wrapped up in yourself that you and your "happiness" or "finding yourself" was the highest value. Much research and experience has shown that seeking your own self-interests above all else is the most destructive and unfulfilling way to live. To jettison marriages or family or morals or values just to "be me" or "find myself" is not a good idea.

I'm Not Saying, "NEVER Do Something That Is Not You"

Second, I am not saying that we *never* do things we're not cut out for or don't like. Again, life is about sacrifice. Contrary to popular belief, we are not entitled to always like everything we do. Working in a job you hate in order to pay for your child's education is sometimes the right thing to do, as is working to support a family. We might go through seasons of life when nothing "feels like me"; but for whatever reason, not doing what we want is required. Sacrificing our own benefit for that of another is a backbone of both character and love.

> Contrary to popular belief, we are not entitled to always like everything we do.

I'm Not Saying, "No *Relationship Should Require You to Set Aside Part of You*"

Third, in relationships, we often have to put parts of ourselves in storage for a season. We can't always be all of ourselves in all relationships or all settings. Making any relationship work requires sacrifice of our rights, freedoms, preferences, and desires for the sake of the relationship. Parents often sacrifice career moves for a season of their child's development. The New

Testament, for example, says that God gives us many freedoms, but if exercising a certain freedom hurts others, we are to give up that freedom for the sake of others or for the sake of a greater mission (see Romans 14:20–22). In the book of Philippians, the apostle Paul goes so far as to say we are to value others *above* ourselves:

> *Do nothing out of selfish ambition or vain conceit.*
> *Rather, in humility value others*
> *above yourselves.*
> *—Philippians 2:3, NIV*

Even when we put aside our personal desires for the sake of people or goals, we do not have to become someone we are not. And beyond that, our efforts at things not exactly "us" can still be fruitful. In fact, in making those kinds of sacrifices, we actually become more of ourselves, true to what we value and love. Purposeful giving actually leads to cheerfulness (2 Corinthians 9:7).

What I *Am* Saying

This never-go-back principle—not doing anything that requires me to be someone else—is about being in touch with who God made you to be and being honest about what you are able to sacrifice in a good way, even a painful way, and what you are not. Jesus said that there is no greater love than to give your life for others. But in order to give your life to others, you must first have a life to give. And sometimes people give up their lives out of pressure from others or because they're in denial about exchanging who they are for something they *think* they want, like Sandy.

> In order to give your life to others, you must first have a life to give.

Sandy was not sacrificing for a purposeful reason. She was in denial about who she could and could not be. The truth is that she did not like most of what she was marrying into. She just liked the idea of marriage, this particular marriage and the status it afforded her. The day-to-day living of that ideal was a different story.

There's an old saying that goes, "Never try to teach a pig to sing. The music is bad and it annoys the pig." God didn't create pigs to sing, and he didn't create us for roles that belong to others.

So, just as we make sure we don't do something that requires us to be someone we're not, we need to apply that same principle to the people and endeavors we allow into our lives. When we consider whether to partner with someone else—hiring her for a job, asking him for help, marrying him or her, depending on him, or even helping her—we should ask ourselves this question: *Is this person really cut out for this?* When we consider getting involved in an activity or endeavor, we need to ask, *Is this decision worthy of my investment of my time, energy, resources, or even life?*

Is this person or thing a suitable fit?

Or am I trying to get a pig to sing?

A Sane Estimate of Who You Are Now

In the last decade, Gallup and other organizations have swept through corporate America with the "strengths" movement. It basically proves, through lots of research, that people perform better when they spend their time and effort doing things they are good at. The person should match the task. The tool should match the work. People should operate in their areas of strength. Dogs should bark instead of trying to meow.

This is an example of what I said earlier about how science and research always affirm the Bible. I love the twelfth chapter of Romans, which says the same things as the strengths movement. In that chapter, God tells us to first commit ourselves to him—the One who made us—in order to find out his will for us. It then tells us specifically what the research says: Don't give in to the pressure from the outside to conform to what the world tells you to be. Then this chapter gives some interesting advice:

> *As your spiritual teacher*
> *I give this piece of advice to each one of you.*
> *Don't cherish exaggerated ideas*
> *of yourself or your importance,*
> *but try to have a sane estimate of your capabilities.*
> *—Romans 12:3, Phillips*

Such sane advice. This is another way of saying *be honest about who you really are and be that person.* Find your gifts and exercise them with full engagement. The Message paraphrase says, "just go ahead and be what we were made to be." If we start with an accurate estimation of what we're good at, and do those things well, we will grow into even more gifts.

When I first knew that I loved psychology, working with people, and theology, I was not ready to do what I do now. I had to be honest about my level of ability and do the kind of tasks that fit me at the time. I started out as an orderly in a psychiatric hospital, not as a full-fledged doctor or psychologist. That first step went well, and I grew. Years later I was a doctor directing hospitals. But we have to start with an accurate estimate of who we really are at the time.

I recently talked to a woman who wanted to be married. But she was very shy in relationships and easily felt rejected. These traits do not prepare a person for a sustainable marriage. And because of these traits, she never dated or put herself out there. So, in order to be her real self and follow the advice of the Romans 12:3 passage, she should not have "exaggerated ideas" about herself—thinking she is ready for things she is not. So, this woman should start small and work on simply talking to men, connecting in safe gatherings, joining a group, and slowly getting ready for a more serious relationship. We apply this never-go-back principle by being where we are, who we are, and starting there.

I recently started reading a contract for a project I am working on. My assistant had been nagging me for a week to read it and sign it. I had been resisting and avoiding the hour of misery it would take to review. Why? *I hate reading contracts*—the minutiae of it all, the burdensome language, and all the details.

I am so thankful that God showed me that I would never have been a happy lawyer—or even a good one, for that matter. It was not me, and I probably would have checked out and failed.

God does not want you to "check out and fail." You are his "workmanship, created in Christ Jesus for good works, which God prepared beforehand so that we would walk in them" (Ephesians 2:10, NASB). Being God's workmanship means that he specifically equipped you for good works that fit who you are. Make sure that you are in touch with the workmanship he did in you and that you are walking in the works that he made you to walk in—not down the wrong trail.

In everything we do, we have to ask ourselves, *Why am I doing this? Is this something God equipped me to do? Is it a sacrifice I am supposed to make? Am I suited for it? Does it fit me? Is it sustainable?* If the answer is no to any of these questions, you better have a very good reason to proceed.

In my experience, people who do well never go back to thinking they can be someone else in order to get something they want. They are honest about who they are or who they truly want to be, and they pursue being that person.

He will be eating curds and honey when he knows enough
to reject the wrong and choose the right.
—Isaiah 7:15, NIV

PRINCIPLE

Never go back to thinking you can change someone.

——

CHAPTER 3

NEVER AGAIN . . .

TRY TO CHANGE ANOTHER PERSON

Ron was a successful businessman, having built many companies and amassed a fortune. He had two daughters and a son, all adults. His daughters had married and moved away—raising families and doing well. His twenty-five-year-old son, Alex, had graduated from college and returned from living in Europe for two years, to begin his career and figure out what he wanted to do.

"So, come to work with me," Ron offered his son. "This is a great company. Your sisters do not want to be in business and someone is going to run it one day; it might as well be you. It is a great opportunity."

Sounded good to Alex, who loved the excitement of it all. The business, the deal making, the stature of the company his father had built. He had long admired what his father had achieved, and now he relished the thought of it all belonging to him one day. It was exciting.

Alex began by working in the different departments—in somewhat of a "floating" capacity—to learn the various aspects of the business. In this time period, he did not have direct responsibility for anything, but was shadowing VPs and gaining a working knowledge of how it all fit together. From there, he would choose a function that he would dive further into, reporting to one of the executives.

Slowly, though, Ron noticed something. As the weeks went on, Alex seemed to come in a bit later, be absent more often, skip some meetings, and not be as fully engaged as the typical employees of the company. Ron wrote it off to this being an orientation period and figured that Alex would be more engaged when he had more important, direct responsibilities.

When the time came for Alex to choose a focus, he chose to dive into marketing, as he was a creative person with a good head for strategy. He was to report to the department head and be responsible for moving certain projects forward.

It did not take long for his boss, Steve, to get frustrated with Alex's lackadaisical approach to work. Deadlines were constantly missed, and Alex did not have the "both feet in" attitude that was typical in this company. Steve talked to Alex about these issues; they discussed how the transition from traveling to work was an adjustment period and that Alex was still figuring things out. Alex seemed to acknowledge his need to step it up a bit, so Steve thought all would be good.

But things did not change. Alex's level of motivation, passion, and work ethic was not what Steve expected of a direct report, nor what Ron would normally tolerate—much less what he would desire from his heir apparent. Steve did not want to get in the middle, so he gradually turned the problem over to Ron, figuring it was between father and son. Soon thereafter, Ron called me.

A Business Saga

"I just don't get it," he said. "This kid is looking at an incredible opportunity, but he's just not grasping it. I try to get him to see how unique this opportunity is—walking into a great company and having the opportunity to take it anywhere he wants—but he just doesn't show the drive it takes. When I was his age, I had started several businesses and was working around the clock. That is what it takes. He seems to want to work only when he doesn't have anything better to do."

"So, what have you tried?" I asked.

"I tell him, 'Son, you have got to get some fire in your belly.' I try to explain to him what it takes to build a business and make it work, how the people look to the owner for leadership and inspiration. How he has to model the kind of energy we want to have inside this company. But then, I don't see much change."

"What happens?" I asked.

"He will seem to get a little spurt of drive, but then goes back to the way he was. He just doesn't seem to want it bad enough." Ron sighed.

We then discussed whether Alex *did* want it badly enough and how much he was willing to put into the job to make it work. And then the hard question: Would Ron be willing to pull the plug on him if he didn't step up?

> Would Ron be willing to pull the plug on him if he didn't step up?

That is when we got to the important moment. Ron said he could not see himself ever doing that and that he would make it his mission to help Alex become the businessman he needed to be to lead this company into the next generation.

"But what if he doesn't?" I pushed.

"It will happen," he said. "I can get him to wake up and see it; and when he does, it will work."

I knew this would not end well.

Although Ron was a successful businessperson, there was an awakening that he had not gone through in regard to his son:

You can't change another person.

But Ron thought he could.

When I interviewed Alex, I was further convinced that Ron's effort to change him was not going to work. Alex was missing two things that are required to head a company like this: hunger and passion. He was not hungry enough to have the drive to do what it would take, and he was not passionate about the business itself. He could have just as easily been selling ice cream, cars, or widgets. He didn't seem to care about the real business and was involved simply because "it was a great opportunity" and it was being handed to him on a platter.

I understood the things Ron was planning to "get Alex to see," but in reality he had already tried these things: paint the vision, expose him to the various aspects of the business, remind him what a great opportunity and business it was, give him some opportunities to get involved and get his feet wet, stay on his case when he did not work hard, supervise him carefully, etc., etc. Ron thought that if he tried harder, he could turn Alex into the business tycoon that he himself was.

The problem was that he had *already* tried, and the more he

tried, the more Alex seemed not to respond in meaningful, lasting ways, and the more frustrated Ron would get. Ron was getting close to resenting his son at a time in life when they should
have been in lockstep, looking at a great future.

I eventually had another meeting with Ron and told him
he had two options: His first option was to continue doing it
his way. He could continue to drive Alex, try to motivate him,
push him to show up, sacrifice, and do all the things that would
be required. I told him I would design a path for that option
if that's what he wanted—and it would include all the important components of recruiting, onboarding, inspiring, development, and the like. But I told him he had already done much of
what I would propose and that in all probability it would not
work.

His second option would be to lay out a very specific path
for Alex, which included clear responsibilities and milestones
and was dependent on performance and objective evaluation.
If Alex decided that he wanted to do it that way and live up to
all of the specific requirements and evaluations to get to each
next step, the opportunity was *his*. But if he did not live up to
the standards of the company and the requirements of the succession plan, then it would be over. It would be up to Alex to
self-select whether or not he wanted to fulfill what was required,
but he could not have either a job or a succession path without
full buy-in.

Ron looked at me for a long time, and at least he was honest.
He said, "I see what you are talking about, and you are probably right. But I can't see myself doing the second option right

now . . . I think I can bring him around. So, let's go with the first one."

I did my best to design a path for Ron to implement but did not hold out great hope for it, as it was missing two basic components. But, it was what Ron desired. It had no defined milestones that Alex could choose to live up to or not, and it had no consequences for not living up to defined milestones. The path his father chose would allow Alex to be halfway engaged while still keeping the benefits of the job. The path included experiences that were designed to engage someone, recruit them to wanting to do the job, and coach them to competency. But I had little confidence that it would produce the results Ron hoped for. I wished Ron luck, and we parted.

I checked in with them some time later; Ron was still frustrated and said the same kinds of things about his son that he had said when I first met them. "He just needs to get into it, and then he will get it," he would say. "He just needs to . . ." on and on. I reiterated what I had said before and wished him well. A year later, I heard that they were still in the same "push-pull" relationship, with Ron still holding out hope.

> We *know* it would be good for them— if they would just "get it." Right?

Sound familiar? It probably does, as we have all either done what Ron was trying to do or have, at least, seen someone else do it: *try to get someone to be or do something they do not wish to be or do.* Yet we *know* it would be good for them—if they would just "get it." Right?

Probably. But *they* would have to get it. And that is the problem.

A Romantic Tale

Stephanie was in love with Kyle. They were great together. The problem was that they had very different definitions of what "together" meant. For Stephanie, it meant being firmly committed and moving toward marriage. For Kyle, it meant being together when he was around, yet his being free to pursue his sports hobbies whenever he wanted—which took him away on lots of fun trips he wasn't willing to give up. He loved her, loved being with her, but at this point in his life, he was not the kind of guy to make their relationship as big a priority as sports.

So they were in a battle. They would be together and it would be great. But then she would want more, he would pull away, she would not like it, and she would begin to exert the pressure. She would say, "I can't see why he can't see how great it would be for us to settle down. We could have it all. Why can't he see that?"

We could have talked for a long time about the reasons he couldn't see it, not the least of which was that he was thirty-four years old and still putting off adulthood in obvious ways. The reasons were certainly there, but naming them would not help. Kyle was not ready to do and be what Stephanie wanted him to do and be. So Stephanie had a similar menu of options as Ron had with his son Alex:

1. She could continue to try to nag, cajole, and control him into changing.
2. She could try to recruit him and influence him, somehow getting him to "get it" by showing him what a great deal she was.

3. She could change her expectations and desires and be happy with the kind of relationship that Kyle wanted to have.

4. She could give him a choice and ask him if he wanted to put both feet in or break up. She would be willing to go to counseling to figure that out, but that would be the bottom line.

In my view, she had pretty much tried the first two, although in all honesty she had not tried a very pure version of the second one. She had not really shown him how great their relationship could be, because every time she tried to do that, she would spoil it with nagging and attempted control because she wanted more. If she had ever done a pure version of just allowing it to be good for a while, it might have worked; but in reality he had probably already seen enough of what "good" looked like with her. For her, number three was just not in her range of acceptable options. I suggested number four.

I won't tell you what happened, but I will tell you the two possible outcomes *if* Stephanie had chosen number four: Kyle decides she is too good to lose, he is willing to give up his freelance lifestyle to settle in and be in a relationship, and she gets what she wants. Or he decides that he does not want to do what is necessary to have her and chooses to go away. In the second scenario, she does not get what she wants with Kyle, *but at least she is free to find someone who wants the same thing she does.* Either way she wins, if you consider being with someone who does not want what you want an unacceptable option.

The Story of *Your* Life

I'm not telling you what happened with Stephanie and Kyle because this is not about them; it is about you. It is about you realizing that you may be in a relationship with someone who isn't listening or doesn't desire to change, or doesn't want what you want for him or her. It's about being in a push-pull scenario where you are trying to get someone to be different. It is about understanding in your own mind that *people who go through this awakening of realizing they can't change another person never go back*. They realize the truth that . . .

> *I can't get someone to do something they*
> *don't choose to do—either because they can't or*
> *because they don't desire to do it.*

The reason? We can never take over another person's freedom to choose. Once we understand this, we never go back to thinking we can. We get in touch with the way God has designed the universe. People are not robots; they are free to choose what they want and what they will do and what they won't do.

When we realize that, we stop trying to do what will never work, which is trying to change people into something they do not want to be or convince them to do something they do not want to do. It never works. While we can influence them, ultimately we cannot change them.

Ron's situation was with a son and in business. Stephanie's was with a boyfriend. The principle is the same, and the situations are endless. Consider relationships that you may have with these types of people:

- A critical person who withholds approval

- An addicted person who refuses to get sober

- An irresponsible person who does not do what should be done

- An employee who is not performing up to standards

- A person who is not investing in a relationship

- A parent whom you wish would be different

- An adult child you wish would grow up and make better choices

- A business partner or coworker who is not matching your effort

God's Way of Dealing with Difficult People

There is nothing in God's Word that says we should not try to influence others to change. In fact it is the opposite: He tells us to try everything possible to get people to choose to change. Nowhere does God say that we should not confront people about destructive or pain-causing patterns. Never does he say we should be okay with people being hurtful or irresponsible. In fact, he says the opposite in many places. He says that if someone is living in a destructive way, we should try to help:

> *Brothers and sisters, if someone is caught in a sin,*
> *you who live by the Spirit should restore that person gently.*
> *But watch yourselves, or you also may be tempted.*
> —*Galatians 6:1, NIV*

If someone is hurting us, we are to confront them and try to help them see what they are doing, even if we have to put on the pressure by bringing in other people to help:

> *"If your brother sins against you, go and*
> *rebuke him in private.*
> *If he listens to you, you have won your brother.*
> *But if he won't listen, take one or two more with you,*
> *so that by the testimony of two or three witnesses*
> *every fact may be established."*
> —*Matthew 18:15–16, HCSB*

God is very clear about what he wants in his relationship with us, and he tells us to be clear with each other. He sees it as a good thing to try to influence each other for good:

> *Rebuke the wise and they will love you.*
> *Instruct the wise and they will be wiser still;*
> *teach the righteous and they will add to their learning.*
> —*Proverbs 9:8b–9, NIV*

So the principle here is *not* that we should be passive or hands-off when it comes to relationships. If we love each other, we will try our best to influence each other for good. God protect me from relationships with people who will not be honest with me about what would be good for me to change! I want people to try to get me to choose to get better. Influencing each other for good is not the issue.

The issue is that we must respect the freedom of others to make their own choices. If we do not respect that freedom, we will do two things. First, we will nag or otherwise try to control them, and they will begin to resent us. Second, we will continually frustrate ourselves as we demand that someone be or do what we wish for them when they do not want to. When they resist, we will end up being angry, shaming, guilt-inducing, or resentful—or all of the above. This path destroys love.

The hard thing is to be honest and clear and to take responsibility for our own wishes, realizing that other people are free to do what they want. We can make our best case, we can even invoke consequences for their choices—like when I suggested to Ron that if Alex chose not to get with the program, he should have to leave the company. Or like I suggested to Stephanie that if Kyle did not choose to be committed to her, she should say good-bye to him and look elsewhere for what she truly wanted. Sometimes clear consequences are the only thing that will cause someone to make a choice—whether it's the choice we want or not. But we can't control whether they make a choice or what choice they make. We can only be the best we can, offer them the best we have, and then allow them to choose.

The Issue of Consequences and Free Will

But notice that those stated consequences are not about making the other person do what we want. In fact, the opposite is true. Consequences are about giving the person the freedom to choose what they will choose, and then our choosing what our response will be in light of their choice. If Alex chooses not to engage in work, Ron's response should be not to continue with someone who is halfhearted. Same with Stephanie. When Kyle and Stephanie get to the consequence stage, neither one should try to make the person they love change. Those efforts have been tried and have failed. Setting consequences in place gives the person a clear choice and sets them free to make it; and then our job is to accept the consequence. We let them know that they can choose a or b. If they choose a, then certain things will happen; and if they choose b, other things will happen. That is clarity and freedom.

> Setting consequences in place gives the person a clear choice and sets them free to make it.

This mind-set does so many good things. It helps you get clear about what you want. It forces you to communicate what you want directly. It keeps you from being judgmental, nagging, controlling, or cajoling—all of which bring about bad feelings in the relationship. And most of all, it preserves the freedom of the other person to make his own choice, something he has had all along, is clearly exercising anyway, and that you are not honoring.

This theme runs throughout the Bible. God says it over and over. Consider the words of Joshua:

But if serving the LORD seems undesirable to you,
then choose for yourselves this day whom you will serve,
whether the gods your ancestors served beyond the Euphrates,
or the gods of the Amorites, in whose land you are living.
But as for me and my household,
we will serve the LORD.
—Joshua 24:15, NIV

In the scripture above, Joshua clearly states what he wants to do and the choice that the others are free to make. He preserves their freedom of choice. Translated to Ron and Stephanie:

- "Alex, if leading this company with full engagement and total commitment seems undesirable to you, then choose for yourself this day what you would like to do with your life. As for me, I choose to invest myself fully here."

- "Kyle, if putting a relationship above your friends and hobbies seems undesirable to you, then choose for yourself the kind of relationship you would like to have. As for me, I choose to be with someone who wants his relationship with me to be a top priority."

Jesus did this same thing in the famous story about the rich man. Clearly, Jesus wanted the rich man to follow him above all else and live forever. But he didn't try to control his choice. When the rich man asked him what he needed to do in order to inherit eternal life, Jesus basically told him that his riches were standing between him and God and that he would have to make his choice. The man chose his riches, walked away, and Jesus let him go:

At this the man's face fell.
He went away sad, because he had great wealth.
—Mark 10:22, NIV

If Ron would let Alex walk away sad because he loved his easy schedule more than inheriting the company, he would do two things. First, he would get out of a power struggle that would never work. And second, he would let Alex feel the loss of what he had given up, possibly prompting him to return once the realization sunk in. The same thing goes for Stephanie and Kyle.

When you realize that you cannot force someone into doing something, you give him or her freedom and allow them to experience it. In doing so, you find your own freedom as well.

Again, this does not mean that Jesus didn't try to convince people to follow him rather than choosing a life or eternity apart from God. And it doesn't mean that Joshua was silent about the importance of following and serving God. Silence or passivity to influence others is not anywhere in the Bible—nor in the research about successful relationships. To the contrary, we are to be very active in trying to *influence*, while at the same time knowing that we cannot *control*. Ultimately we have to recognize that others are free.

As vernacular wisdom says:

You can lead a horse to water, but
you can't make him drink.

How happy the people are who avoid frustration by not trying to get a horse to drink water when it has no thirst or doesn't like water. Show people the water. Show them how cool and refreshing it is. When they are dehydrated, tell them that water would help them. Tell them how much you would enjoy drinking water together. Show them what it has done for you. Burp loudly. But realize that you can't make them drink. That is something they will do only when and if they want to. Remember . . . they are free to choose.

"Never go back" to thinking you can force someone into anything. Repent from trying to control others. You will be glad you did.

Fear of man will prove to be a snare,
but whoever trusts in the Lord is kept safe
—Proverbs 29:25, NIV

PRINCIPLE

Never go back to trying to please other people.

CHAPTER 4

NEVER AGAIN . . .

BELIEVE THAT YOU CAN PLEASE EVERYONE

It was several years ago, and I had just spoken at the Willow Creek Leadership Summit. After the session, I was walking down the hall with Willow's founder, Bill Hybels. We were talking about the incredible growth and reach of Willow and appreciating all of the great work it was doing. It was touching millions of people around the world.

At the same time, Willow had its very vocal critics. The mission of Willow was to reach people who had no interest whatsoever in God and bring them to a full commitment to Christ. Their growth and results were so powerful that Harvard Business School studied the church to see how it had accomplished what it did. But as Willow Creek grew, some voices in the Christian world came out against them, critical of their style.

Willow had put aside much of the stuffy, judgmental, goody-two-shoes feeling of church for a more welcoming atmosphere. They called their style "seeker friendly." That meant you did not have to be "religious" to go there and get something meaningful. Even if you were totally "irreligious," you could feel comfortable there and hear a message about a God you had never considered, possibly because you had been turned off by "church."

But, the "church lady" types around the country did not like that. (Remember her from *Saturday Night Live*? She symbolized everything we have experienced about judgmental, rigid church communities.) They blasted Willow and Hybels for being "shallow," not being "biblical," and a host of other criticisms. What many of the critics were really upset about was that Willow was not doing things the same way they were. Sad reasoning.

Right before my visit to Willow, I read a negative article about Willow by a church leader and heard a subsequent radio interview blasting Willow and throwing out negative "charges." The discussion had been all over Christian media. So I asked Bill what he thought of it.

His answer caught me by surprise.

"No, haven't seen that one. I don't pay attention to that stuff. Too many other things to do."

Really? I thought. *You just got blasted by this big-time preacher guy, and it didn't register?* So I asked him.

"Really? You just let it go?"

"Pretty much. I have to do what I feel God is telling me and Willow to do and not worry about all of that junk. People are going to say what they are going to say."

Not long after, I had another experience with a Christian leader who had been criticized by someone, and his response was quite different from Hybels's. He went into full-blown defense, calling a lot of people, challenging the opinions, trying to persuade others that he really was a good guy. He was anxious about people's impressions of him and was working hard to change their opinion. He *had* to have them like him.

The contrast was sharp.

Contrasting Ways to View Criticism

First, the difference in the amount of energy the two men expended on the threat was amazing. One basically yawned and paid no attention to his critics, and the other could do nothing *but* pay attention. It dominated the second man's attention and consumed all of his energy. It put him on hyperdrive and derailed everything else he was doing. He was running around, calling people, trying every way he could to protect his image. He spent a lot of steam on image control, while Hybels and Willow marched steadily forward toward their purpose.

> *Pure and simple,*
> *the difference is one of* **offense** *versus* **defense.**

Second, Hybels and his dedicated people did not allow critics to derail the purpose they believed God had called them to. But the other leader's purpose was completely sidetracked when he was criticized, and he instantly began to play defense. Defending himself or his mission to others had suddenly become the "main thing." He was no longer leading nor was he in charge. Instead, his critics were. He was off track, out of focus, depleting his energy and drive. The bottom line is this: *his critics gained control of how he spent his time and energy simply by criticizing him.* What a diversion.

Third, neither Bill nor Willow was opposed to feedback or criticism. In fact, they welcomed it, even sought it out; they did research on it and actively evaluated how effective they were in their mission. They believed that feedback—negative or positive—helped them become the best they could be. Not being distracted by other people's opinions was about something very, very different than not listening to feedback. It was about not needing to have everyone *like* them or think they were right, or even good. It was about not needing to *be* what others wanted or needed them to be. And it was about not needing to *do* what others wanted them to do. And the end result of laying aside all these burdens was that they could be open to criticism yet not defined by critical people or governed by other people's agendas.

> They could be open to criticism yet not defined by critical people or governed by other people's agendas.

The difference in the two approaches was that . . .

One man believed he had to please people—all people; while the other focused only on pleasing God.

Certainly, if you are human, you care whether people like you or not. It matters to anyone who has a heart. Only the most emotionally and relationally cut off people have zero interest in whether others like them or feel positively toward them. We all have a human need to be loved by others, and we all enjoy positive appraisals. Our entire beings are wired that way from infancy on. Smile at a baby, and you will get a different response than if you frown at him. But that does not mean that everyone who frowns at you for the rest of your life should all of a sudden become your master.

Reaching for the Possible, Not the Impossible

Successful people eventually go through a doorway that is essential to making their personal lives, as well as their professional lives, work: *they realize that they do not have to please everyone or have everyone like them.* In fact, part of what fuels that realization is the bigger realization that not only do we not *have* to please everyone, we *can't*—even if we wanted to. It is *impossible*.

The reality is that everyone likes something different, has different agendas, tastes, interests, beliefs, and experiences. It is literally impossible to make everyone happy, even within your closest circle of friends. You are going to like and choose some things that some people won't like or choose. That is reality. Basically the only way to avoid upsetting anyone is to believe, say, or do nothing at all. Not a good option. Once you realize that, and really, really get it, something happens.

You give up what is impossible,
and begin to focus on what is good.

Playing Offense

Once you get that it truly is impossible to please everyone, you begin to live purposefully. You begin to play offense. You start spending your time and energy on things that bring meaningful results, rather than on the impossible goal of making everyone else happy. Spending energy to get results is "playing offense." A nice thing about playing offense is that your fruitfulness will actually please people who allow you to be you, provided you are pursuing truly good and fruitful things. The ones who want you to be or do something other than what you are cut out for won't always be pleased—but when we understand our end goal, to do good, this matters a little less.

And once you begin to play offense, you'll discover the difference between playing offense and being offensive or offended. Some will take offense at your not doing what they like or want; but that's the time you need to stand firm, knowing that you can't please everyone. As we used to say on the golf course, "Every shot makes somebody happy."

> Once you begin to play offense, you'll discover the difference between playing offense and being offensive or offended.

In a memorable movie scene, a son makes a life decision that his father does not like. His father says indignantly, "How could you do this to me?"

The son looks at him and says, "Dad, I am not doing this *to* you. I am doing this *for* me." Big difference. He was not being offensive; he was playing offense, doing what he was called to do.

He realized that he was not being offensive nor was he offended because his dad did not approve.

Choices Always Divide

Successful people realize that just because someone is unhappy with them does not require that they give up their purpose, fold their cards, or change. They realize that making some people unhappy is just part of the deal—and they keep going. I once heard Tony Blair say that when you realize that *every decision divides*, it really helps. It is just part of life. When you turn to the right, there will be some who want you to go to the left, and vice versa. It is the nature of making choices. *When we accept that every decision divides, we quit trying to do the impossible, i.e., pleasing everyone, and we begin making the right choices, knowing that our choices will divide.*

> Successful people realize that making some people unhappy is just part of the deal—and they keep going.

Psychological research and experience tell us that people-pleasing is not a formula for happiness or success. Happy people do not compare themselves to others or overly concern themselves with others' opinions of them. They are directed from the *inside*—their personal values and convictions and staying true to themselves is an inner compass they will not violate. Research shows that people with intrinsic motivations—motivations that come from their own hearts—are the successful ones. The people who reach goals are the ones who do what they themselves have decided to do, from their own hearts, not because of pressure from others. The Bible agrees with the research when it says, "A man's heart plans his way, but the Lord determines his steps" (Proverbs 16:9, HCSB). Our hearts and *God* guide us, not the opinions of others.

This does not mean that successful people ignore correction and input from others. Far from it. As we saw with Bill Hybels, the most internally directed people are the most open to feedback. Why? Because they do not fear it. They welcome it and use it to become better directed—internally. When it is good, they make the feedback part of them, which is way different from trying to live up to the expectations of others. As they make changes based on feedback, they are not trying to please the ones who provided the feedback; they are trying to become better versions of themselves.

It turns out that seeking people's approval is one of the things that God warns us about over and over. Proverbs 29:25 says that "the fear of man is a snare." Paul says that if he were seeking the approval of men, he would no longer be a servant of Christ (see Galatians 1:10). Jesus unpacks this further and gives a stronger warning, in the strongest language:

> *"Woe to you when everyone speaks well of you."*
> —*Luke 6:26a, NIV*

Reasons *Not* to Please Everyone

There are so many reasons not to please everyone that it is hard to list them all. We've talked about how seeking others' approval steals time, energy, and focus. But beyond that, Jesus shows us that it would be even worse if you were able to pull it off!

1. You Would Have to Be Multiple People

If you were able to make everyone like you, by definition, you would have to be more than one person! You would need to be one person with one group to meet their expectations and another person to meet another group's expectations. If you try to keep parents, friends, church members, and everyone else always liking you and approving of everything you do, you will have to be several contradictory people living in one body! This is the definition of a duplicitous person and the epitome of what psychologists call a lack of identity. It leads to all sorts of emotional, relational, and psychological problems. As the Bible puts it, this kind of person is "unstable in all his ways" (James 1:8, HCSB). And psychological research affirms this over and over.

2. You Would Make the Wrong People Happy

And, worse than that, if you are making everyone happy, you are also making some of the wrong people happy! You'll be trying to please people who are judgmental or controlling or arrogant, people who require others to do what they want them to do before they extend approval. So, to keep hurtful people happy, you must do some things that are not good in the long run. You have to make some bad choices to keep these people smiling.

For example, if you lead a team of people and have one person on your team who is self-centered or controlling, that person will only be happy when you make decisions that meet her individual interests or agenda. But when you need to decide something that is best for the entire team, that person will be unhappy if she does not get what she wants. So if your goal is to keep her happy, you must make decisions that are not good for the team.

> *The people who are hardest to please*
> *are often the most self-centered*
> *and are only happy when you do what is*
> *good for them—*
> *and that usually is not good for the whole.*

So, when God tells us that we are in big trouble when we are pleasing everyone, he gives us one of the most important principles to making life work. And the people who do make life work, *make decisions based on what is best*, not on who is going to like it. Below are some examples of wise but unpopular choices:

- Choosing a profession that is right for you, even if your family or friends would like for you to do something different

- Standing up to hurtful behavior, such as addictions or abuse, even if the addict gets upset

- Leading teams and organizations in the way that best reaches the vision, even if some people do not get what they want or do not like your approach

- Parenting your children well and being able to say no to the child who wants to do something that is not good for him

- Refusing to do unethical, immoral, or illegal things that someone in power, such as a boss, friend, or even family member wants you to do

- Telling someone a necessary truth about behavior that is hurtful to themselves, others, the family, or the team

- Making decisions that are right for your own family unit, even when it displeases parents or in-laws, such as where to spend a holiday or go to church

Handling Unpopular Decisions

Recently I met with two different large family businesses in the same week. The contrast between them was stark. One of them was seriously divided by dysfunction; the other was united through strong, ongoing relationships.

In this particular week, both families were making some

significant decisions that would affect other family members. In the dysfunctional family, the father had been avoiding dealing with an issue because people in one of the family units would not like what had to be done. For a couple of generations, he had tried to make everyone happy and had allowed his relatives to think that if they were not happy, something must be wrong. They had learned to believe that being unhappy with a particular situation equaled being mistreated. Fearing their displeasure, he had been paralyzed for quite a while, and it was costing the company and the rest of the family. But now he realized that the issue could no longer be avoided and that continued avoidance would make matters even worse. So he finally made a decision and called a meeting—excluding the affected family. Then he made the mistake of instructing those present not to let the affected family unit know about it. He said, "They will not be happy about this, but we have to do it—so just keep it to yourselves. They will probably find out at some point, but don't tell them now."

I cringed. I had the feeling that a key never-go-back awakening was needed in this family. The thought went through my mind loud and clear: *This is not going to end well.* Not only was the affected family not going to like it, they would feel betrayed and kept in the dark—*all because the father was afraid of making them unhappy.*

It was easily apparent why this family had all the pain it did. From division, to conflicts between adult siblings, to competitiveness, they'd created much unnecessary turmoil over the years. Why? They avoided honest discussion about difficult decisions because someone would be unhappy. When they were forced to deal with serious issues—like in this instance—they would use secrecy and triangulation. And that would further divide the family. They had not learned the principles that not everyone can always have their way and that the group needs to work together for purposes larger than themselves. They had never learned what my kids learned in preschool: "You get what you get and you don't get upset."

> They had never learned what my kids learned in preschool: "You get what you get and you don't get upset."

Right after that I met with the other family, who had almost the exact same issue to deal with. It involved the use of some family resources and a decision that was going to limit them. Like the first family, it was a decision that had to be made and that was unpleasant. A few members of the family were not going to like it.

But unlike the first family who was afraid of not pleasing everyone and kept difficult decisions secret, this family leader did exactly the opposite. The father said something like this: "Okay, this is what we have to do. But do not talk about it until I have had a chance to let the others know. They are not going to be pleased with this, and I want to make sure they hear it from me directly and not find out some other way. It is going to be very difficult for them to accept, so I want to let them know right up front."

My eyes misted. It was like I was seeing the true meaning of holiness acted out in real relationships—a moment when we get a glimpse of the way God designed life to be. It was an example of love: *people caring enough to be honest with one another, even if the other person was not going to like what they heard.*

This father did two things well. First, he was not afraid to do what was best and needed to be done, even if some would not like it. But second, he intentionally took the news directly to those who were not going to like it. He risked not pleasing them. He risked their not being happy with him. He loved them enough to tell them the unwanted news directly.

He loved them enough to risk their disapproval.

Then I saw a big picture. The fruitfulness this family experienced in so many areas was no accident. They had done well because they had done things the way God designed life to be lived. They made decisions based on what was right, what was best for everyone, and not necessarily what would please everyone—as difficult as that was.

Pleasing Father—Or Not

One of the hardest decisions I ever had to make was the year I graduated from college. As I've mentioned before, I had been an accounting and finance major, thinking if I did not pursue a career in the golf world, I would go into business, like my father, or perhaps law school. But halfway through college, I had a deeper faith experience, and I felt God was clearly telling me to switch my major to psychology and pursue a career in that field. My father was not telling me the same thing.

The first bump came when I changed my major. He was not ballistic about it, but he wondered what in the world I could possibly do with a psychology degree; it seemed so impractical to him. But through a lot of discussions, I convinced him that there was work to be found if I went to graduate school. Still, I could tell the path was not clear to him, and I remember feeling a bit out over my skis. Not only was I unsure about where this was all headed, I was not confident that I had his approval. I knew that he put high value on a college education that prepared you for life, and he had always wanted me to be well prepared. To him, it seemed that I might be squandering my opportunity. Nevertheless, I continued my new path.

The bigger bump came when I graduated. All of my friends were going to work for great companies and pursuing bright futures that seemed very well defined. I was not one of those. It was clear to me that God was leading me into psychology of some sort, but I had a lot of questions about the field and exactly what I could do. I wanted more clarity, and I wanted to understand what I was getting into. So I decided I needed some real, hands-on experience.

The problem was that you can't really do much with an undergraduate degree in psychology. It takes a master's or PhD to work in the field at a professional level. So my father's concerns had proved *true*. I was a college graduate, but I was unprepared to do much in my chosen field. All I knew was that God had led me to this point and that I had to continue to follow his leading. What to do?

Through a lot of prayer and events, it became clear. I was

to go to work in a psychiatric hospital to learn more about the field. But the only job I could get in a psych hospital without an advanced degree was as an entry-level orderly. That would be great experience, since besides delivering food trays and taking vital signs, I would get to observe a ton just being there, sitting in the groups, and helping the staff implement goals and treatment plans with patients. I would learn so much about the field. It would be a great learning and clarifying experience.

There was just one problem. It paid about three dollars an hour. Not enough to live on and not enough to convince my father that my expensive college education had not been squandered. I would have to take on extra work just to pay my bills, even with a college degree. My accounting-major friends were getting high-paying jobs and joining private country clubs. I was collecting half-eaten breakfast trays served to anorexics who didn't want them. I was not yet the college grad who would make my dad proud.

When I told him what I was going to do and what I would be getting paid, he just shook his head and said something like, "I hope you know what you are doing." To his credit, he did not interfere or threaten to disown me, but I do remember feeling that I was not making him happy. I had always wanted my dad to be proud of me, and this did not seem like a good launch. It was a hard decision—doing what I thought I needed to do versus doing something that would make him proud.

Somehow I stuck with it and took the hospital job. I went in extra early every morning to eat the breakfasts that the anorexics did not want; getting free food was a nice perk. I scrounged and did carpentry and other work at night and on weekends to pay for life.

But through this time, I continued to do something I will always be grateful for: *I pursued what I knew I had to do, even if it was not what others thought I should do.* I knew that it was right for me before God.

The lesson I learned from this time changed me. I came to the very important realization that sometimes you can't do what others want you to do. You have to march to a different drummer—the purpose that God has for you. You have to do the right thing, even when you might not please everyone else.

After that year and what it gave to me, I can never go back to letting people's expectations dictate my course. That time literally prepared me for the rest of my life's work. I do not think I would be doing what I am today if I had not had that year as a college grad working in a below-poverty-line job. It was one of the biggest blessings I have ever had. It made my entire career go in a different trajectory.

My father did not try to stop me and didn't give me a hard time, and I am thankful for that. He honored my choices and allowed me to experience the consequences. He did not bail me out of the difficulties my three-dollar-an-hour job presented. But I fully understood that my pursuit did not live up to his expectations, and that was a hard but great lesson for me. It was one lesson in learning to never go back.

Choose the Right Master

The Bible tells us that we have one master—and one master only. We will all answer to God for our lives and the choices we make. On that issue, the Bible is very clear: "Each of us will give an account of himself to God" (Romans 14:12, HCSB). I like the way Solomon puts it:

> *When all has been heard, the conclusion of the matter is:*
> *fear God and keep His commands,*
> *because this is for all humanity.*
> *For God will bring every act to judgment,*
> *including every hidden thing, whether good or evil.*
> *—Ecclesiastes 12:13–14, HCSB*

There's a huge "awakening" lesson in the passage above—a principle that can change the direction of your life.

We tend to see accountability to God as being all about judgment, but in reality, accountability to God is an incredible guideline in the people-pleasing department. The direction of our lives can literally be saved if we live life mindful of this truth.

Since we will ultimately answer to God for our decisions, it behooves us to remember that *he* is the one we need to please. If ever we think of forgoing what is best in order to please another person, this is the truth we need to fall back on. If pleasing God is our compass, and if we know we will answer to him, our path will be much clearer.

When I look back, I know I made the choice to change

my major and work at a job where I could barely pay my bills because God had led me to do it. Knowing this helped me to say no to the pressure to pursue a path that others deemed better. God is the one who counts, and if we live to please him, we will always make better decisions and will be better in the end.

Think about this the next time you feel pressure to please someone yet feel that the right decision is one that they do not like. Picture yourself at your life review with God having a conversation that goes something like this:

God: "So, why did you not take the opportunity I offered you? It was exactly what you wanted."

You: "I know. I really wanted to and knew it would be best for me and others, but you know how upset _____ would have gotten if I did. It would have been awful."

God: "You are right. _____ would have gone through the roof and would have been really upset with you. And, I have a meeting with _____ later . . . in exactly three years, two months, six days, seven hours, and thirty-three minutes. At that time, I'll be talking to _____ about his [or her] tendency to get mad at people when they did not please him [or her]. That is a streak of selfishness that he [or she] never gave up, and I will take care of it. But that is _____'s life, not yours. You are responsible for your own choices. You are responsible for your own decisions and _____ is responsible for how he [she] responded to you. Don't worry, I will be bringing that up. Not your problem, then or now. But, the fact that you chose to give in to him [or her] is your problem, and now I want to show you the life that you gave up by living the life that other people wanted. Watch that screen over there. . . ."

Then you see what could have been if only you had not tried to please someone else.

Frightening, isn't it? Remember, whoever you are trying to please is accountable for his own life, and you are accountable for yours. Whenever you live for someone else, he controls two lives, his and yours. Yet we are the ones who will answer for the life that is truly ours—the only one God gives us.

> *Staying mindful of that makes you a partner with God,*
> *instead of with the people who want to control you.*

Living to please God will bring you to the best version of yourself, the one he created you to be. It is not about being "judged" or condemned by God, but about choosing the best possible master in all the universe.

Please him and live the best life possible for you. Otherwise, you might have to watch it as a movie of what you chose not to live while you were pleasing someone else.

No discipline seems pleasant at the time, but painful.
Later on, however, it produces a harvest of righteousness
and peace for those who have been trained by it.
—Hebrews 12:11, NIV

PRINCIPLE

**Never go back to avoiding short-term pain when it leads
to long-term benefits.**

___

CHAPTER 5

NEVER AGAIN . . .
CHOOSE SHORT-TERM COMFORT OVER LONG-TERM BENEFIT

I used to think that "sluggard" meant lazy, that it meant someone just did not want to put out the effort required to do something or get something, or that they were "inactive." I thought lazy people were couch potatoes—not doing much that takes effort.

But after years of working with successful people, as well as with people who were stuck, I noticed something. *You can be very active and also very lazy at the same time.* I learned that "lazy" does not mean "couch potato" or "inactive" at all. In fact, some of the "laziest" people are very, very active. How can that be? This dilemma gets us to the heart of this chapter's "awakening."

I began to do some research into the meaning of the word "sluggard" as it is used in the Bible. I saw that it is closely tied to the word "indolent" and other meanings that basically refer to people who want a life that is devoid of "pain." So you can be lazy, or a sluggard as the Bible puts it, and still be very active. But in all of your energy and activity, you will still be lazy about doing anything uncomfortable or that involves pain. So I began to understand something:

The true definition of "sluggard"
is someone who avoids pain.

Here is the truth: Once successful people know they want something that requires a painful, time-limited step, they do not mind the painful step because it gets them to a long-term benefit.

I cannot overstate how many times I've seen this confirmed in real life—from the simplest things to the most difficult. It is just a law of the universe:

Anything of value has this rhythm to it: **pain first, payoff later.** *If we face the pain early, the payoff will come.*

And the converse is true as well:

If we avoid the pain now, the payoff will never come.
And more pain will.

Living out this principle is one of the most fundamental differences between successful and unsuccessful people, both personally and professionally. Successful people will go through the brief, time-limited, painful step to get to what they want, and unsuccessful people will not.

I saw this in working with successful people and unsuccessful people side by side. The successful people would always do the hard thing, and the unsuccessful ones would not. The unsuccessful people

People who avoid pain will not get what they want. Period.

would put it off because they didn't want to go through the pain. I began to see that people who avoid pain will not get what they want. Period.

I knew this truth in the people I worked with, but then I began to see it in the Bible as well. Over and over again, I saw the theme: *pain first, payoff later.* No pain, no gain. Death before resurrection. Discipline before strength. Investment before return.

So, stated simply, here is the "I will never go back to" principle:

> *I will never go back to avoiding something*
> *I know I need to do just because it is going to be painful.*

This is so obvious that I almost feel elementary in writing about it, but it is a principle that is avoided every day by very smart people. I see it over and over in the difference between people who get what they want in life and those who don't. The ones who succeed go through the short-term painful step, and the ones who don't, don't.

The Principles in Action

Let's look at some common examples:

Sally was dating a guy whom she had become attached to, but she knew she didn't want to be with him long-term. There were some things missing in the relationship, and some things she did not want to deal with for the rest of her life. Yet she put off the inevitable breakup for two years. She continued in her present reality rather than taking steps to get what she really wanted. Why would she not take those steps?

She knew they would be painful.

————

Richard owned a business that was in a bad location. He knew a move would be required if his business was ever going to reach its potential. But every time he considered a move, all he could think about was the six-month disruption while he relocated—informing customers, not being able to do business as usual during the move, conflict with some employees who would not like the change, the hassle of updating insurance, mailing lists, vendors, etc. Each time he thought of the pain involved in the change, he put it off. Unfortunately, avoiding the pain also meant not gaining the growth he desired. Why could he not bring himself to make the move?

He knew that it would be painful.

————

William and Rachel lived in a home they had outgrown. It needed a remodel. They could afford to do the work financially, and if they did it, they would have the home that their family needed and that would serve their larger mission in life, which included using their home to minister to others and to have guests and gatherings.

But when they would think about it, all they could see was living through the painful period of the remodel. It might take up to a year, they figured. They would either be living in dust and tarps or have to move into a nearby rental while the work was being done. Life would be uncomfortable. Why didn't they make the move?

They did not want to go through that painful period required to get to the home they desired.

————

Jennifer was a salesperson who loved helping people and wanted to be in the healing profession. But when she looked into it, she found that it would require going to night school to get her prerequisites and go through a nursing program, and this would require a couple of years. She did not relish the thought of being a student again—she would have to work as well as study. But on the other side of that time-limited pain was the career she dreamed of. Yet she did not pursue her dream. Why?

It would be a season of discomfort and relative chaos for her life.

————

Compare those situations to these:

Sarah had gone back and forth through a few breakups with her boyfriend, Todd, because of a big difference in their values. She loved him, but after a few rounds of breaking up and getting back together again, she awakened to the reality that this would never be what she wanted long term. The only thing in between her and what she truly desired was going through the pain of a final "good-bye" and sticking to her decision, even though she would feel sad and alone for a time.

She went through the painful breakup, and eight months

later she met the man she had been waiting for and dreaming about for a long time. If you asked her, she would certainly "never go back." The short-term pain of the breakup was more than worth the new life she'd found.

———

Paul owned a small neighborhood restaurant but wanted to move it to a new location with much better street traffic and larger space to accommodate more tables. It was hard, and he had to juggle many things while he went through the transition, shifting to a take-out model for a period of time while the move was happening. It took a lot of hand-holding with customers and resulted in a pretty disruptive life for a time. But when the new place opened, he tripled his business. Hard to go through, but he would "never go back" to the way it was. The short-term pain was well worth the long-term benefit.

———

I visited my friends Sandra and Jake for dinner in their rented cubbyhole of a home that they had just moved into. I had not been in touch with them to know much about the move, so when I got to their new place, I asked why they'd moved.

"We had just outgrown the old house, but we did not want to move. So we are adding a few rooms and doing a remodel. It is going to take about eight months, so we moved here in the mean-time. It is a pain to make it all work, but it is going to be worth it."

About ten months later I went to a party at their newly remodeled home, and it was so much better. They loved it, and if you asked them if they were glad they put up with the eight months of stepping all over each other in the cubbyhole, they would say "absolutely." They had gone through the short-term pain to get what they knew they needed.

———————

"How's it going?" I asked Steven.

"I can't even begin to tell you," he said. "I had to go through some very hard times, but now I feel the most alive I have ever felt."

"What do you mean?" I asked.

"Well, remember when I told you I was making the move to get my financial advisor licenses so I could become a certified financial advisor?" he asked.

"Yes, I do," I said. "You were worried about how much work it was going to be and about the shift in professions."

"I was, and now that I have completed it, I can tell you my concerns were legitimate. The change was very hard, but it was the best thing I ever did. I love my work now. I have my licenses, got hired by a great firm, and am actually doing the work I always wanted to do. It is not easy, but it is exactly what I want to be doing."

Another way of saying, "I would never go back."

———————

So what is true about all of these situations? *They were all alike in the beginning.* People who were in similar situations knew it was time to take a step; they were certain of what they needed to do to get where they wanted to go. And they all knew that the step was going to involve a period of specific, time-limited one-time pain, disruption, or discomfort.

The thing that is *not* true about all of them is that the first group did not do what was needed to get to the result it desired. Not because they couldn't do the work or break up with a guy or relocate a business or move a family to a rental or find a new employee or take the courses needed to qualify for a different kind of work.

What they could not find in themselves to do was one of the most important qualifications of reaching success in any aspect of life, personal or professional: *They could not go through the short-term time-limited one-time painful step required to get to where they wanted to be*—a breakup, a move, a different living situation, a new hire, a time of study and coursework. The short-term discomfort. That was the only difference in the ones who got there and the ones who didn't. The ones who succeeded were willing to go through the painful moment required to get what they desired.

> The ones who succeeded were willing to go through the painful moment required to get what they desired.

I remember my youngest daughter, Lucy, having a splinter in her foot when she was about five. She wanted to resume playing in the yard with her sister and friends, but her foot hurt every time she put weight on it. She came to me for help.

"No problem, Luce," I said. "Let me pull it out, and you will be on your way. It is not deep, but it's poking you every time you run. After I pull it out, it will be fine."

"Okay, Daddy," she said.

I sat her down and went to work. As soon as I touched it, she screamed and cried. "NO! Don't touch it. It hurts."

"I know, but it will only be for a second," I reassured her. Then I grabbed her foot again.

"OUCH!!!" she yelled. "Don't touch it there, it hurts."

"I know, Luce, but I have to if you are going to be able to play. Just sit still for a minute," I said.

This was not working. We went around and around, not getting anywhere, until I pulled the Daddy trick.

"Okay, just let me look at it," I said.

"Fine, but don't do anything," she said.

I very, very softly lifted the splinter without her knowing it, secured the tweezers, and yanked.

"OWWWWW!" she screamed. "Don't touch it, I said!"

"Okay, I won't," I told her. "It's gone. Go play."

"What?" she said.

"Yep, all done. Get out of here," I said.

She put her foot down—no pain—and sheepishly grinned. She took off, and that was that. It bugged me because I wanted to give her an "I told you so" lecture to teach her that sometimes you have to go through a moment of pain to get to the place you want to be, but I figured that would have to wait for another time. Maybe she will read this book one day.

But the truth is the truth. A moment of pain can lead to a long time of relief, if we are willing to go through what successful people go through all the time—face a season of pain, disruption, discomfort, effort, or something that hurts a bit. Then we can have what we want.

Learn the Principle Once and for All

There are two ways to look at what we have just talked about. The first is to see each situation as a stand-alone challenge, like the challenge of a breakup or a move. The temptation is to see that process as a one-time step to success that only applies to that particular situation.

While it's true that each situation has to be dealt with on its own, there is a bigger lesson here. The reality is that the people who make the choices that lead to long-term benefit have become the kind of people who know that taking painful steps to get where you want to go is a *necessary part of anything good*. They have learned never to go back to thinking that pain and discomfort can be avoided in the pursuit of long-term benefit.

What we need to repent of is the "pattern" of avoiding discomfort that keeps us from what we want and what God has for us. The truth is that Sally, Richard, William and Rachel, and Jennifer were not stuck in only this one situation. If we had the video of their lives, we would see that this was not the first time they had resisted holding their breath and taking the deep dive to go through some pain to get where they needed to go. It was a *pattern*, and the pattern is what they needed leave behind.

The truth is that they would face other situations that would require them to do something painful, and they would avoid that short-term pain as well. Only when they recognized that they had a *tendency* to avoid the immediate hurt necessary to getting what they desired and determined to endure the short-term pain would they move to where they wanted to be. Their life-pattern was "pain avoidant," and unless that changed, they would never make progress.

Life experience and the Bible both tell us about this life-certainty: pain always comes before pleasure, investment before profit, exercise before health, study before a passing grade, discomfort before healing. Once people learn this truth, they "never go back" to thinking they can, or should, avoid the hard moment to get to the Promised Land. God's message is clear: Go through the right kind of pain first, and you will get what you desire. The New Testament puts it like this:

> *Therefore, since Christ suffered in his body,*
> *arm yourselves also with the same attitude,*
> *because whoever suffers in the body is done with sin.*
> *—1 Peter 4:1, NIV*

In another place we read,

> *No discipline seems pleasant at the time, but painful.*
> *Later on, however, it produces a harvest*
> *of righteousness and peace for those who have*
> *been trained by it.*
> *Therefore, strengthen your feeble arms and weak knees.*
> *"Make level paths for your feet," so that the lame*
> *may not be disabled,*
> *but rather healed.*
> *—Hebrews 12:11–13, NIV*

We could go on and on about how clear the Bible and life are about this lesson, but one thing I have seen over and over again: Successful people "get it." And once they do, they never go back to avoiding a little pain to get where they want to be. They "arm themselves" with that attitude, as the verse above says. They see it as a weapon to fight the battles of life; they have the attitude and willingness to get the splinter out that is keeping them from being able to play. They willingly lean into the short-term hurt that stands between them and what they want.

The biggest example of this is Jesus himself. The Bible tells us that he went through the suffering of the cross to get what he wanted, which was to provide forgiveness for you and for me:

> *And let us run with perseverance the race marked out for us,*
> *fixing our eyes on Jesus, the pioneer and perfecter of faith.*
> *For the joy set before him he endured the cross,*
> *scorning its shame,*
> *and sat down at the right hand of the throne of God.*
> *—Hebrews 12:1–2, NIV*

He went through the suffering of the cross that was required to get what he wanted: our forgiveness. And the message in this verse is that we must run with that same perseverance in our own lives in order to reach the callings God has for us and realize the dreams he has put in our hearts. Here is the rule: suffer first, and benefit later. We can't avoid short-term pain if we are going to get where we really want to go. No pain, no gain. So, the lifestyle change required is this:

*Never go back to a pattern of avoiding short-term pain
that is in the path to long-term benefit.*

We must turn from our "inner sluggard," the one who would like to avoid the moment of pain when the splinter comes out or the disruption of life that gets us where we want to go. Repent from hoping for a life with no painful moments and arm yourself with the same purpose Jesus had: "to suffer" to get to the place that God has for you. Whether that suffering is required to avoid a destructive pattern of sin or reach a dream, repent from thinking that there is any other way. Do the hard thing first, and the good will follow. Embrace the hard moment to get to the Promised Land. Death before resurrection.

Successful people willingly lean into the short-term hurt that stands between them and what they want.

Is there pain to be had in making anything better? Absolutely. Is it worth it? Absolutely. As many, many successful people in relationships and in business have told me, making the change was a lot harder than they thought it would be, but as soon as it was done, they asked themselves, *"So why didn't I do this sooner?!"*

What step of pain are you avoiding that will lead to where you want to be—in your personal or professional life—if only you will embrace it?

Who can say, "I have kept my heart pure;
I am clean and without sin"?
—Proverbs 20:9, NIV

PRINCIPLE

**Never go back to being taken in by someone or something
that looks perfect.**

—

CHAPTER 6

NEVER AGAIN . . .

TRUST SOMEONE OR SOMETHING FLAWLESS

I had been asked to help an organization choose their next president, and they had narrowed the search to the last candidate. In the meeting before the final interview with the entire executive team, the search committee was giving the group the update on why they had come down to this particular candidate. The reports were glowing:

"He increased the growth of his last organization by huge multiples."

"He is so well rounded; he possesses all the gifts we need."

"You should hear him present his vision—it is incredible."

"He is good on his feet, so quick and smart."

The accolades went on and on. I could not wait to meet this guy. I shared their enthusiasm.

When the group interview with him began, I had to agree—he was impressive. His account of what he had done in past positions was enviable. Lots of stories of accomplishments, victories, and turning things around. He had passion, drive, and commitment. Charisma.

When he shared how he would approach the current situation of this business, he had some excellent insights concerning the market realities, new technologies, and strategy. I was impressed.

I was also becoming uneasy.

Something did not feel quite right. It was a feeling I have had in many situations, and it was one of those never-go-back principles that was giving me the uneasy feeling: *The guy was too good.*

He seemed too ideal. Perfect. Invincible. Above it all. Always victorious and successful. I had a queasy feeling that I was getting slimed. It all felt a bit greasy, like it was all too good. So I asked a question: "So tell us a bit about your weaknesses—some failures you have had. Tell us about some areas where you need growth. And tell us how those particular weaknesses might affect this position or this organization," I said.

He was silent. It seemed like hours, but was just moments.

"What do you mean?" he asked.

"I just want to hear about some of your weaknesses and how you see them impacting this position," I repeated.

Again . . . silence. He was like a deer caught in the headlights.

Finally he said, "I guess my biggest weakness is that I am such a driver and achiever that I sometimes leave people behind."

I was getting nauseated. I said, "I'm sorry. That sounds like another strength. Can you tell me about a weakness?"

Suffice it to say, his responses did not get clearer as we went on. He danced around a bit, but never got to anything that felt like a clear weakness or an awareness of how he would deal with that weakness or how it would affect his work.

The interview went on and then ended. We excused him, and the group immediately chimed in.

"He is the guy."

"Perfect for what we need."

"I wish we had had him two presidents ago."

"Let's make him an offer."

Then they turned to me. I basically said, "Please put me on record as saying that this guy is trouble and is the last person you want to hire."

They looked at me like I was crazy.

"Why?" they asked.

"Because according to him, he has never failed. And I do not want you to be his first experience at failure. He has no awareness of anything he does not do well or any flaw or weakness or any way in which he has ever failed. He has nothing to learn. In his view, he has arrived. To me, that speaks of an incredible amount of arrogance, blindness, narcissism, denial, and more. He might have done well in the past, but when he hits any difficult situation that he cannot handle, you are going to have a problem. He won't be able to see how he needs to change or grow or take ownership of anything he needs to do differently. He will always try to look good, and my guess is that he will try to hide anything that makes him look bad. I would stay as far away from him as I could," I said. "I vote no."

> "He will always try to look good, and my guess is that he will try to hide anything that makes him look bad."

It was not a comfortable moment. They pretty much all

looked at me and said, "Thanks for your thoughts; we appreciate them. But we think he is the guy, so we are going ahead."

It's a long story, but the summary is they hired him, and in the next two years he took the organization down a path to failure that took them five years to recover from. And most of it was because he was presenting an all-is-well picture to the board of directors, saying how well things were going—a picture that was much better than the reality. He failed to communicate the real problems in the business because he did not want them to see the truth. In his stance of trying to look ideal to others, he refused to face real problems; and the company lost money while he portrayed an image of success. In short, his life at the company was a continuation of his perfect interview— giving the impression that everything was great when in reality it was not.

I had to do it. When it all surfaced, I said, "I told you so."

When we talked about it, they asked, "How did you know? He seemed so awesome."

"That was the problem," I said. "He seemed 'too awesome.' Nothing wrong with accomplishments or a great record, but a person who is unaware of his weaknesses, faults, failures, or struggles is a person who is out of touch with reality. And I did not want that quality in this company. I wanted a leader who is not so intent on looking good that he cannot own what is wrong with the business or himself—even if the truth paints him in a less-than-perfect light.

> "I wanted someone who was more invested in *doing* well than *looking* good."

I wanted someone who was more invested in *doing* well than *looking* good."

They nodded. My hunch is that they would "never go back."

What Are You Attracted To?

Remember the saying: "All that glitters is not gold." Yet we humans are often drawn into the dangerous deception that someone or some situation is perfect, wonderful, ideal, and without blemish or problems. And for some reason we believe it. We think we have finally found paradise. The perfect person, the perfect place, the perfect job, the perfect church, the perfect boss, pastor, friend, or mate. Only to discover that underneath the perfect hair, Dracula lurks.

It's natural for us to be drawn to things and people that appear "incredible." We love excellence and should always be looking for it. The Bible refers to it as virtue, or goodness. We long to be in relationships and settings that are good, excellent, fruitful, and high performing. Love goodness, God says, and pursue it (see 1 Timothy 6:11).

Loving goodness is not the problem.

We *should* pursue people who are great at what they do, employees who are high performers, dates who are exceptional people, friends who have stellar character, companies that excel. No need to go for worms. Go for the best.

So I am not telling you to be suspicious of all that is good, strong, beautiful, and of high quality, or to not require it. What I am telling you is that when someone or something looks too good to be true, he, she, or it is. This world is imperfect. Period. No one and no thing is without flaw. When we realize that, we will be much less vulnerable to being seduced by people and situations that appear perfect—with no faults or side effects whatsoever. When we are deceived by the portrayal of perfection, we set ourselves up for a great fall.

The awakening, or realization, to be had here is something you've heard before:

When someone or something looks too good to be true,
he, she, or it is.

Seek Goodness Coupled with Healthy Humility

So my message is this: Continue to be on the lookout for goodness, but make sure that goodness is coupled with its sister and driving engine—humility. People who have healthy humility are not self-deprecating and don't put themselves down in order to appear non-arrogant. The opposite is true: They know their strengths and how to articulate them.

For example, if I were interviewing a potential president for a company, I would want her to be self-confident and tell me what her strengths are and what she thinks she could accomplish. But I would also want her to be humble by being in touch with reality about herself and her situation.

I want a presidential candidate who says, "I am really good at strategy, and sometimes I have a tendency to get too caught up in the future and overlook the details of the operations. I have had to learn that I need to round out my team with someone who keeps the details in front of me all the time and makes sure that we deliver on the milestones. To do that, I hire a very strong COO." This is someone who knows who she is and can identify her strengths and weaknesses. I can trust this kind of person to take care of her weaknesses and protect me from them, so I do not have to protect myself.

Humility is not self-depreciation. It is reality. It is being in touch with what the Bible tells us over and over: *We are all imperfect*. The book of 1 John says it this way:

> *If we claim to be without sin,*
> *we deceive ourselves and the truth is not in us.*
> *If we confess our sins, he is faithful and just and will forgive*
> *us our sins and purify us from all unrighteousness.*
> *If we claim we have not sinned,*
> *we make him out to be a liar and his word is not in us.*
> *—1 John 1:8–10, NIV*

I love this passage! What I love most is that it says that when we think we are totally cool and without fault (sin) "*we deceive ourselves.*" Notice that it does not say, "We deceive others." Think about that in terms of the people you know who are in denial about their own imperfections. They might be deceiving themselves and think they have no faults, but others are *very aware* of their issues! In fact, there is a direct correlation: The more someone is in denial of their own issues, the more others talk about them! They are visible to all but themselves.

Think of your circle of friends or extended family or work-place. People who think they have it all together or are above everyone else or never have any struggles are annoying! They are the people who cause the biggest problems for others because they are unaware of their own problems. They want to appear perfect and as if they have it all together, and as a result, they continue in their glaring weaknesses that everyone else sees, are affected by, and talk about.

But God gives us a very different alternative that enriches our relationships and contains the promise of always getting better:

Be honest and own it.

The passage above says that if we "confess" our imperfections, God will not only forgive us but he will help us get better. He will "purify" us. The way to get better is *not* to try to look better than we are, but to be honest about who we are and allow God to take our weaknesses and make them better. That is the key to growth.

James puts it this way:

> The way to get better is to be honest about who we are and allow God to take our weaknesses and make them better.

Therefore, confess your sins to one another
and pray for one another,
so that you may be healed.
—James 5:16, HCSB

If we admit where we are wrong, where we have failed, we can be healed and grow—we can get better. It's impossible to get better if you don't have a problem!

Uncommon Words That Make a Big Difference

Let's take a minute to dive a bit deeper into the meanings of two words that can make a huge difference in our lives: "confession" and "sin."

Back to what I said earlier about the word "repent." Although it is a religious word and has significant negative baggage wrapped around it; in reality, it can save our lives. "Repent" means to "turn away from." Said another way, it means to "do something different than what is not working." Duh . . . what an insight!

"Confession" and "sin" have also gotten much negative press. But to understand these words can save us from so much pain, and that is why God gives them to us.

First, let's look at "confess." Literally, the word means to agree with or acknowledge. That's it. It does not mean to grovel in a confession booth before an old critical man; it just means to agree that "this is an issue. I agree—I have a problem." "Or, I did that, and I shouldn't have." Once we agree that something is an issue, God says, "No prob; I forgive you and can help you with that." Just come to the dentist and agree that there is a cavity, and then he can fix it. But if we won't acknowledge an issue as an issue—confess that we have a toothache—we cannot find help.

> God says, "No prob; I forgive you and can help you with that."

Now for the word "sin." The word literally means to miss the mark. It means that we did not hit the bull's-eye. We missed it. We did not get it right. Who among us has not missed the mark? Missed the bull's-eye? Every single one of us has missed it.

But some put on an image of never missing the mark. Always getting it right. These people try to come across as perfect.

Buying into the Façade

Two things happen if you buy into their façade.

First, you will be in for a rude awakening. No one is perfect, and if you were counting on a certain person being so, you will be greatly disappointed.

Second, when something goes wrong and you call this person into account, you get only denial and defensiveness. Good luck trying to resolve a problem.

A better way? Do not desire or trust "perfect" people or situations. Seek out people who have incredible goodness as well as an ownership of their lack of goodness. Such people are working on flaws, learning from them, and desiring to do better. Look for people who are "real" about who they are, not trying to appear perfect. Those are trustworthy people, and God is on their side:

> Seek out people who have incredible goodness as well as an ownership of their lack of goodness.

God resists the proud, but gives grace to the humble.
—James 4:6, HCSB

Repent from looking for perfection and, instead, look for "good and real." In your personal life, in your relationships, and in business, move toward those who have admirable qualities and strengths, but who are also real about their struggles, weaknesses, pains, and faults. If you do that, you will be with people who own their problems and work on them—so you don't have to.

Good and Real, Not Perfect and Ideal

Woody Allen said, "I hate reality, but it's still the best place to get a good steak." Said another way, "Real people may disappoint me, but they are the only ones you can have a relationship with." Why is that? It all goes back to the Bible.

The book of Genesis says that God created a perfect world. It was ideal. The Garden of Eden was "paradise."

But then, sin, or "missing the mark," entered into the world. Humankind turned against God and his right way of doing things. Ever since then, the world has been an imperfect place with imperfect people. Those who accept this reality can find great goodness and satisfaction in this life; those who don't are always thinking that paradise, or perfection, is out there somewhere—in a person, a job, a city, or a situation. So when a seemingly perfect person or situation presents itself to them, they fall for it. Suckers for an immature fantasy of life as Disneyland.

The problem is that the Bible tells us a reality: paradise, or perfection, in this world is gone forever. We can never go back

(Genesis 3:24). Now, our only alternative—other than denial—is to embrace living life in an imperfect world, as imperfect people, with imperfect others. If we can accept that, our eyes are open to the imperfections in ourselves and others, and that gives us a keen vision for the real goodness as well.

But naïve people are caught up in the fantasy that Eden is still available, and because of that, they are open to great seduction by people and situations that look too good to be true, and in fact, are. They are nightmares.

Our culture has tabloids with stars who look as if their lives are ideal. They find the perfect mate—their "soul mate"—whom they have always been looking for. They live in perfect houses. They have perfect lives. People spend all their money and time trying to be like them—getting liposuction and buying clothes to emulate these remnants of Eden.

But go to the supermarket the next month and the same stars have just split with their perfect "soul mates" and the tabloid headline reads, "The Breakup: What Really Happened?" Or, they lose their perfect mansions to a drug addiction, or outrageous behavior destroys everything that looked so good.

If we will embrace the "real" instead of the "ideal," we can often find experiences of heaven on earth.

Don't buy into the Hollywood version of perfection or even the church version. Many times Christian groups can appear as if they have it all together as well—as if their spiritual lives hold no struggle or pain or defeat. That is not the story of the Bible. God is real, not a fantasy, and he invites us into a real spiritual life and a real life on this earth. The good news is that if we will embrace the "real" instead of the "ideal," we can often find experiences of heaven on earth.

So be on the lookout for good and real, not perfect and ideal. Look for people and situations that have great goodness but are also aware of their imperfections and are working on them. If you do that, you will find rich, fulfilling people, situations, employees, employers, friends, churches, and the like. There *is* real goodness in this world. But if we are looking for perfect, we will have to go to another world altogether. And that is a fantasy.

If you are dating, look for a person who is aware of his or her issues and struggles, as well as all the things you are attracted to. If you are looking for a church, find one that has a community of fellow strugglers along the journey of life. If you are looking for a circle of friends, find one where the people are real, not trying to look perfect or ideal. Look for people who are humble and able to laugh at themselves—those who are aware of themselves and are not troubled by their own kookiness. And by the way—strive to be that kind of person yourself.

Repent from the pursuit of "perfection." Whether trying to *be* perfect or looking for it elsewhere, repent. Once you do, you'll "never go back."

And the God of all grace, who called you
to his eternal glory in Christ, after you have suffered
a little while, will himself restore you and make you
strong, firm and steadfast.
—*1 Peter 5:10, NIV*

PRINCIPLE

Never go back to losing the big picture.

CHAPTER 7

NEVER AGAIN . . .

TAKE YOUR EYES OFF THE BIG PICTURE

During the economic crash of 2008, I worked with several companies as a leadership consultant. CEOs were dealing with horrible circumstances in pretty much every industry. Whether on Wall Street, in real estate, retail, or industries, the crash affected every business. Leaders were trying to cope with multiple issues, and one of the most important was keeping the morale and motivation of their people moving forward in the midst of a horrible time. Many high performers were bottoming out.

In several companies, I conducted focus groups to learn how employees were dealing with the crisis. The focus groups had three purposes: First, to find the ones who were doing well and keep them moving forward and further empower them. Second, to figure out *why* some were still performing well so others could do the same things. Third, to help turn around those who needed help.

Thrivers versus Strugglers

In several industries, a few themes emerged. There were very real differences between the ones who were still thriving and the ones who were hitting bottom, between those who were winning and those who were not. One of those distinguishing factors is the subject of this chapter:

> *The thrivers kept the big picture in mind,*
> *while the strugglers were caught up only in what*
> *was going on at that moment.*

One of the first places I saw this was on Wall Street. I began to notice a glaring difference in many stock market executives and financial advisors, depending on their past experience. Now remember, both those who were striving and those who were not were very, very high performers—industry leaders and award winners. They had achieved incredible heights of success.

The difference was often this: *Some of them had been through market crashes and difficulties before, and some had not.* Either because of age or years in the business, this was the first time some people had seen catastrophe hit. For them, the world had changed and this was the "new normal." *Life was over as they knew it, and would never return. It was virtually hopeless.*

When times had been good, they were succeeding in every way, and their brains had been trained to think there was a simple formula for success: You do certain activities and you will succeed. The work is predictable. Profits happen. You can depend on it.

Now, their tried-and-true strategies were not working, and

they were lost. This new way would be permanent, they reasoned; the good times were gone. It was over. Hopelessness set in, energy waned, and their brains basically stopped working.

But there was another group that *was* thriving, finding new strategies and doing well. Some were even having the best year they had ever had. What was this difference?

Some had been in the business long enough to have experienced the crashes of '73 and '87, and others had been through the bubble crash of 2000–2002. Those who had gone through those downturns had a perspective that was very, very different:

They saw this crisis as one scene in a much longer movie.

In the simplest of terms, they knew from experience that markets go up and markets go down—sometimes *way* down. That is the business. They knew it was time to do the things you do in a down market, and they did those things with vigor. And they won. Why? Were they smarter? More strategic? No.

They won because their brains were still working while the others had shut down.

As they say, "It's all in your head." Literally.

Intended for the Long Term

Basically, it works like this: God wired our brains with the capacity to see the long term, not just the moment—the movie, not just one or two scenes; the whole book, not just a chapter; the whole day, not just lunch.

God wired our brains with the capacity to see the long term, not just the moment.

When we see any event in terms of a longer story, our minds put that event into a different context—the big picture. We know that this moment is not all there is. It is just one moment in a bigger picture, and we focus on the big picture while still in the small moment. When we do that, we do well. We function better emotionally and perform better in our lives. Our brains are wired with the capacity to do this. Seeing the big picture does three things:

First, it gets us out of the subjective present feelings of "everything is bad" and lifts us into the objective narrative of where we have been, where we are, and where we are going. We realize it is only one day in an entire week, one week in a month, one month in a year, and one year in decades. When we have this perspective, our emotions change; and when our emotions change, our brains change as well.

Second, it changes the moves that you make. This perspective gets you doing things that will lead to the bigger outcome you desire, instead of simply reacting to how you feel in the moment. (Not burning bridges, for example.)

Third, seeing the big picture allows you to learn the lessons of the present. In the Wall Street example, the overcomers' brains took advantage of their God-given capacity to put this crash in perspective, calm down, and not lose hope. They kept working, finding activities that fit the moment and also put strategies in place for the next season—when things turned around. While some brokers wanted to jump off a bridge, those with the big-picture view regrouped and made even *more* investments—in the right things, at the right time, while prices were down. Instead of thinking, "It's all over," they asked, "What behaviors does this particular scene require?" They got moving and did different things—the things required in a crisis as part of a longer-term picture.

For successful people, no one event is ever the whole story.
Winners remember that—each and every day.

Keeping the Main Thing the Main Thing

I was talking to a CEO client of mine who was excited about an upcoming gathering of friends and coworkers. The event was an anniversary celebration for the founding of their company, and she was going to be honored for some big accomplishments. But now, there was a snag. She found out that one of the attendees would be someone who had tried to get her removed from the company—a former board member.

This person was no longer with the company, but had almost "destroyed her life" in the process. This CEO's feelings about this were huge. And beyond that, since what had happened was well known, she felt a bit hurt that those in charge of the event had invited this person and put her in this situation on her big day. It was going to be very awkward and very public.

When she called me, she was extremely upset. The whole thing had left a bad feeling in her gut, and she was considering not participating. It would be too hard, she felt, and she just did not want to go through it.

I listened, heard her out, and really understood her feelings. Parading the entire conflict in such a public way was almost unthinkable.

She vented, going back and forth over the possible scenarios—including gossip and news coverage—and had a lot of heartburn.

Then, all of a sudden, her entire tone changed and she brightly said, "You know what? I think I am going to say, 'Wonderful,' and just go through with it like the planners have decided. I won't bow out. I am going to go and make it a great day."

"How did you decide that?" I asked.

"I just saw the bigger picture. I realized that what I want is for the people and the company to thrive, and for the culture to be stronger than petty, political differences. Instead of making an issue out of this, I am going to go with it—for the sake of the bigger picture. If I do, it will be good for what we are trying to build," she said. "My life here is not about this event; it is about what we are building."

I actually felt I was in the presence of greatness. The reason successful people do better than others was right before my eyes: *They keep the big picture in mind.* Then they do the activities that are required by the whole movie and not just the one scene.

My client followed her plan, and the event went well. She had her moments and had to process a few things as she went through it, but she accomplished what she wanted. She preserved what was important for the big picture.

Because she saw the big picture, her *emotions* changed, her *actions* changed, and *how she learned* changed. Let's look at all three.

The Big Picture Changes How We Feel, Act, and Learn

Changes in How We Feel

When something significant happens, our emotional state can change. And when we keep our eyes on the "little picture"—the right now—our emotions can change in a negative way.

Take the stock market crash mentioned earlier. Because it affected people's real lives—their retirement balances, college funds, savings, and other assets—they went into emotional overload. Their financial security was threatened.

When we go into overload, the part of the brain that kicks in to protect us puts us into a state of "fight or flight." We want to react, push against, or get away. We feel angry, fearful, aggressive, anxious, or consumed with self-loathing. When we or someone we know feels like this, we see that emotions overtake judgment, motivation, and every other aspect of functioning.

Besides feeling these reactive emotions, we can also lose hope. Everything begins to feel "bad" and like it won't ever get better. We experience the emotional reactions that researchers such as Martin Seligman have labeled the Three P's:

- Personal

- Pervasive

- Permanent

For example, if a spouse has a midlife crisis and leaves his wife, she feels hurt. Emotionally, she might see the external event as "personal," making emotional conclusions about herself. In her emotional state, she interprets her husband's leaving as meaning that "he left because there is something wrong with me. I am not attractive enough, attentive enough, exciting enough" or some other "enough." She sees his leaving as a lack on her part, not a problem on his end.

Her emotional reaction then becomes "pervasive." She feels, "Not only does my husband think I am not good enough, people at work feel the same way too, and so do my social circles. Really, I am not good enough anywhere. I am a loser all around." It goes "all bad" in her mind.

Third, it goes "permanent." She feels like "it will always be this way." The future looks bleak and hope goes away. By this point, she is losing energy, getting depressed, feeling anxious, and is going down for the count. She might get impulsive and act out in some way that will not help anything, or she might just throw in the towel and retreat. Either way, the event has colored everything about her emotional state.

All she can see is what is going on in the present, and it becomes her whole life. It is everything. She might even feel that she has nothing to live for anymore.

But if she can step back and see the big picture, her feelings begin to change. She sees more than this one scene of the movie of her life. Her life is bigger than this one tragedy. As she slowly regains the big picture, she begins to feel that perhaps there is hope for her—and a future. And as her feelings change, she is able to change her actions, too.

Changes in How We Act

When she emotionally realizes that the pain her spouse inflicted upon her is not personal, permanent, or pervasive, she is able to take action. She joins some friends in a group at her church and they connect with her pain—validating her pain and not denying it at all. They do not try to talk her out of how painful it is. They listen to her and walk through her pain with her. They support her, and this connection slowly begins to help her "get into her right mind." As the trauma feelings subside as a result of their support and time, she gets out of the emotional state of being overwhelmed and begins to think more clearly.

> In her emotional state, she interprets her husband's leaving as meaning that "there is something wrong with me."

She realizes that although this is painful, it is not her entire life. Her children need her. Her extended family is there for her. Her work is fulfilling. Her faith is strong, and God promises to take her through anything. She is able to change her actions in these areas because her feelings of hopelessness have changed.

Changes in How We Learn

She also learns more about why men do this, and she finds out that there is more to the picture than she thought. She learns that her husband's actions have to do with his own narcissism and selfishness, his need for instant gratification and self-reinforcement, his lack of maturity, his immature dependency on women, and a bunch of other things that have nothing to do with her "attractiveness."

She joins a group for separated wives and learns that in the bigger picture, there are possible scenarios that might actually end in reconciliation. She learns that even though she cannot determine her husband's choices, she can choose to respond proactively instead of reacting out of her immediate pain. She learns that this is one scene in a much larger movie.

She also learns to think about what outcome she wants for *herself*—not just in relation to him but also for herself as her own person—her whole life. She learns that she wants to be healthy and thriving, no matter what he does or doesn't do. She realizes that he is not in control of her well-being or future. She begins to do some things that will ensure that she gets where she wants to go. She joins another group, gets a good therapist, connects with her friends, and begins to work on herself in a whole new way for her future.

As she regains the big-picture view of reality—about herself, others, the world, and her future—her brain changes in several ways. It goes from reacting to responding and planning. It puts the event into a timeline of a much bigger story. When we see the bigger story, we see a future with things to be done, actions to be taken. When we see the bigger story, we are more objective in our thinking and less subjective in our "global" emotionality. We are able to learn in whole new ways that broaden our perspective and bring well-founded hope. In other words, we realize that this is just one event, not "the whole thing."

A Day in the Life

One of the biggest examples of people *not* taking the long view is in sports. As a competitive golfer who has followed golf my whole life, I find it fascinating to see the big-picture versus little-picture dynamic play out in major golf tournaments, such as the US Open or the Masters. Some players know how to handle the ups and downs of the four-day grind of these tournaments and have a chance of winning. Others always seem to find a way to choke. They may have been leading the tournament, even into the final nine holes, but in the end they lose. Why? Often, it's because they lose sight of the big picture.

They are floating along doing well, beating everyone else— obviously possessing the talent to win. Then they hit one into the lake. That one shot, that one occurrence, turns into a big global event. "OH NO!!!!!" their brain thinks. *I AM LOSING IT! Whatever made me think I could lead this tournament? I am not good enough to win a US Open!! And it is not just my driving; my putting is not feeling so great, either. And I bet this is not the only hole I am going to hit the ball in the water. I will probably do it on the next hole also. I am losing it . . . it's all slipping away.*

Then their global emotions take over, and their actions change. They get rushed, they lose concentration, and they begin to make real behavioral mistakes that do, in fact, change the "movie." It does not end well. And all of that happened because they lost the big picture.

Contrast that with a great champion who does not choke. When he hits a bad shot early in the tournament, or even has a bad first day, he reasons, *I am bummed about today, but this is a*

four-day tournament. There is a lot of golf left to be played. Then
he reviews the problems he had that day. Maybe his stance was
off a bit, so he fixes it and sets a course record the next day. Now
he is leading the tournament.

Or perhaps the player is leading on the back nine of the last
day and then hits a bad shot. She treats it as one bad shot or one
hole, instead of feeling like she is "losing it and it is all slipping
away." It was one shot, period.

In the financial crash, when the brokers I worked with
regained the "big picture," things began to change. They put the
crisis in the perspective of a long narrative about the market and
the economy and how they perform. They were bummed, but
not in despair. They realized that this was one event in a much
larger career.

The Bible gives an amazing picture of seeing the bigger view.
When the apostle Paul went through severe persecution—much
worse than a financial crash or a bad golf game—he said:

> *We are pressured in every way but not crushed;*
> *we are perplexed but not in despair;*
> *we are persecuted but not abandoned;*
> *we are struck down but not destroyed.*
> *—2 Corinthians 4:8–9, HCSB*

Paul knew how to look at the big picture and keep things
in perspective. And as my broker friends began to see things in
perspective, their emotional state changed, they began to act differently, and they learned to adapt. Just like the deserted spouse

whose emotions calmed down and who began to act strategically and get healthy, the brokers who got the big picture did the same thing. They began to meet with their clients and get them involved in the big picture, which in turn calmed down their clients and kept them from doing something impulsive and destructive, like pulling out all of their money and putting it in a cookie jar. Or changing brokers. Instead, they looked at their bigger picture goals, reminding them of what they were trying to accomplish—like retirement by a certain year, college paid for by a certain time, etc. When they put their losses into that bigger picture and worked within historical timelines, people began to see that their goals were still within reach, even with this setback. As we have seen, the market did recover. Those who took the long view recovered, too.

The brain is wired with the capacity to live out the big picture and to manage the little pictures along the way. The little pictures are meant to serve the big picture, never the other way around. Everything we do is part of the bigger story of our lives. Our lives are going somewhere, and the end really does matter. When we adjust the big picture in reaction to one scene, we lose control of our lives and the story we are building. One market crash, and someone abandons investing and becomes a hoarder. One relationship crash, and someone gives up on love for a lifetime.

> The brain is wired with the capacity to live out the big picture and to manage the little pictures along the way.

Keep the big picture in mind.

God's Big Picture

One of my favorite verses in the Bible is when Jesus said,

> *"In me you may have peace.*
> *In this world you will have trouble.*
> *But take heart! I have overcome the world."*
> *—John 16:33, NIV*

Paraphrased, it says this: When troubling events occur, take heart—and for good reason. It is just one event. The bigger picture is that God has overcome the world and all of its trouble, and he will help you overcome this trouble, too. Our journey is much bigger than any one event, and it's a journey we can successfully complete in the end. We will be victorious if we stay close to God and follow what he tells us to do,

The Message puts a portion of the John 16 passage (31–33) like this:

> *Jesus answered them, "Do you finally believe?*
> *In fact, you're about to make a run for it—*
> *saving your own skins and abandoning me.*
> *But I'm not abandoned. The Father is with me.*
> *I've told you all this so that trusting me,*
> *you will be unshakable and assured, deeply at peace.*
> *In this godless world you will continue to*
> *experience difficulties.*
> *But take heart! I've conquered the world."*

This is exactly what we are talking about. Jesus warned his disciples not to get caught up in the drama of the moment he was captured and not to lose heart and run away. He told them to remember the big picture—no matter what happens. God is God! He has it all under control! Jesus assured his followers that he would not be abandoned by his Father and that the capture would not cause him to lose heart. Rather, he would have peace knowing the bigger picture.

I like the way the psalmist puts it when talking about the person whose trust is in God:

> *He will never be shaken.*
> *The righteous man will be remembered forever.*
> *He will not fear bad news;*
> *his heart is confident, trusting in the Lord.*
> *His heart is assured; he will not fear.*
> *In the end he will look in triumph on his foes.*
> *—Psalm 112:6-8, HCSB*

The Bible's message is that we are all part of a much bigger story than our own lives, and that the big story of our lives fits into the big story of God's life. It goes something like this:

"Be human and don't try to be your own god. Let me be God, and you be you."

God created us to love him and one another and enjoy all of the wonders of life. It was his gift. All he asked is that we remember that He is God and we are his creation, subject to him. In other words, "Be human and don't try to be your own god. Let me be God, and you be you. I, the Creator, will supply life, and you, the created one, are to live it and enjoy it responsibly."

But we decided against his plan and chose to reject him and be our own gods. Each and every one of us. The result was that a world apart from God and his ways went crazy, sort of like unparented children. Lost, fighting, afraid, trying to figure it out, using drugs and other methods to cope with the pain, and unable to have stable relationships. Theologians call it a "fallen world," meaning that this world fell from its created perfection to the sad state of affairs we see today. Not that all of the good was lost; we still have beauty. But all of it, even the most beautiful sky or relationship, is subject to pollution.

But God did not want us to stay this way, so he came back to us, like a jilted lover and said, "I want you back. Come to me. If you do, even though you will still live in a fallen world with many troubles, I will be with you and will lead you to victory. First, you'll have victory over how this life has affected you because I will be your Father. Next, you will learn to function and deal with all that this life can throw your way, no matter how bad it is. But the end game is this: The journey you go through in this life will prepare you for *real* life, the next life, where there will be no fall from perfection and where life will be as I originally designed it. Your responsibility now is to not let this life get to you, but to take my hand and use what happens here to prepare you to live in the next one. Learn how to love, learn how to use your talents, and learn how to overcome this sinful world just as I have overcome it. Keep the big picture in mind; stay with me. We are headed somewhere very, very good."

The Re-created Life

God's story is not about any one event. No matter how we are being hurt in the moment, when we think like Jesus and stay connected to God, we realize that no matter what today looks like, God has not abandoned us and he will re-create our lives as we submit to him. God is with us.

We see God's re-creation in us in life's little instances, as well as in big ones. For example:

- The CEO earlier did not respond negatively to the guest who had almost ruined her life, but instead remembered the big picture of what she was trying to build in the company. She thought of the outcome she wanted and acted in ways that would bring that about.

- The spouse who does not react to a slight or hurt in an equally destructive way—returning "evil for evil"—but instead overcomes "evil with good" and reacts to the hurt in a way that can actually repair the relationship. This person keeps the big picture in mind, realizing that even though his feelings were hurt, he will still be married later today and refuses to carry the slight into the rest of the night.

- The single who is rejected in a relationship but does not interpret it as meaning she is not worthy of love, or that there are no good ones out there, or that she will never find anyone and will always be alone. Instead, she realizes that this is just one event in a journey of finding the right person, while handling the event in a positive way. For instance, using a failed relationship to learn why it did not work, why she might have chosen someone who was not capable of love, or what she might be contributing to the problem that she needs to change. She keeps the bigger picture in mind and learns from the event.

- The person who loses a job but decides it will not be the end of his career. He sees it as one event, and then he makes the changes necessary to adapt to the economy and makes moves to change the outcome of the movie. He might learn a new skill or a new business model or whatever it takes. But he knows that God is with him and is leading him and that God can bring good out of every event if we stay connected to him in our love relationship (see Romans 8:28).

- Even the person who loses a loved one to a premature death. The most devastating of losses can make anyone feel like "life is over." Losing our deepest attachments can shift our entire view of life, for they strike at the very fabric of our hearts. But people who go through death and mourning well and recover and find life again are those who keep the bigger picture, the longer narrative of life, alive. They realize that no matter how bad this is, God does have a future for them and that he can still be trusted. Their trust in God grows to the point that they can say with Job, "Even if He kills me, I will hope in Him" (Job 13:15a, HCSB).

So What's Happening with You?

So how does this relate to you, right now? Is there someone in your family or work or church or community who is making today difficult? The lesson here is to "keep the end in mind" and respond in a way that will preserve what you want to have happen in the end.

You don't want to give this person the power to ruin your family, career, job, office, church, or friendships; yet that's exactly what might happen if you react badly and lose the big picture.

Think about what you want to preserve—the relationships larger than this one person and your own emotional and spiritual well-being. Then think about what actions are warranted in this situation to get to that end result, no matter what it feels like today. The one who takes the long view is the one who thrives, no matter what happens along the way.

The plans of the diligent lead to profit
as surely as haste leads to poverty.
—Proverbs 21:5, NIV

PRINCIPLE

Never go back to taking the easy path
and failing to do due diligence.

CHAPTER 8

NEVER AGAIN . . .

NEGLECT TO DO DUE DILIGENCE

"So, how long have you lived here in Nashville?" I asked our server at the restaurant.

"About a year, and I love it, but my daughter and I are about to move," she said.

"Oh, really?" I asked. "Why are you moving if you love it?"

"Because my boyfriend lives in Chicago, and I am moving there to be with him," she said. "A long-distance relationship is hard."

"That's true. Must be pretty serious?" I asked.

"Yes, we are perfect together," she said. "We are a great match."

"Cool. How long have you guys been together?" I asked.

"Two months," she said.

"You have been dating for two months? How long have you known him?"

"For two months," she said. "I met him this summer."

"And you are going to move to be with him after only knowing him for two months?? Really?" I asked, a bit startled.

"Yes. He really is great," she said emphatically.

"Wow . . ." I said. "Wow . . . wow . . ." I just didn't know what else to say. "Why did you move here?"

"I had come here to finish my degree in nursing," she said. "But I didn't start the new semester because I would have had to pull out early to move to Chicago, so I decided to try to go to school somewhere there next January."

"So you could be with him?" I asked.

"Yes. I didn't want to start school and then move later to be with him," she explained.

I just nodded.

She went away, and my friend Dr. John Townsend and I just looked at each other, shaking our heads.

When she came back, I couldn't refrain.

"I don't know you," I began, "but I have to be honest with you. You changed your whole life to pursue your passion here, you love living here, and you had a plan. Then you meet someone and are instantly ready to give all that up, move to Chicago, not knowing what you will do there, after knowing him for only two months? That seems *really* fast."

"Oh, I don't think so. We are perfect together. We are such a good match. I am sure this time," she said.

"This time?" I asked.

She went on to tell me about her previous marriage and how that had ended. But now she was "sure."

"Weren't you *sure* when you married the first one?" I asked her.

"Yes, but he turned out to be not so good. I did the right thing to get out of that," she said.

"Maybe you would do well to have a little more time to be 'different sure' this time before you uproot your entire life after two months of knowing someone," I said, totally surprising myself with how direct I was being with someone I had known for five minutes. What a pain of a customer I was.

"No, I am sure. I can tell," she said.

We volleyed a few more times about the whole topic of taking time to know someone well before making big decisions, but it was clear: she was *sure.* She was on a mission to get to Chicago, and no mere restaurant customer was going to slow her down, even if I was a psychologist and had written several books on the topic.

"Well, you might be the exception," I said. "Some people meet and make a decision very quickly and have things turn out well. It does happen. But in my experience, that is the exception, not the rule. Much more often, when people fall in love and make a big decision before they actually know what they didn't know, they end up with a lot of regrets.

"My totally unsolicited advice? He might be right for you; but if he is, he will be just as right a year from now as he is now. So, my suggestion is that you take some time to get to know him better before you totally uproot your life."

"I know that makes sense; but if I wait, then I will have already started school here and I don't want to change schools."

Then came the killer response.

"I know that makes the most sense; but if I wait, then I will have already started school here and I don't want to change schools. I would rather move and start there," she said.

"And if he is not in the picture a year from now, is Chicago where you want to be living?" I asked.

"No, I mean, I could live anywhere. But it is not my first choice. I would rather live here. That is why I moved here, but he can't move because of his work, and I can go to school there," she explained.

"Well," I said. "I hope it works, but if it doesn't, I hope you like Chicago, because it sounds like you are going to be digging in pretty deep there. And if you and he do not work out, that is where you are going to be."

"I know," she said, "but it will work."

We talked a bit more, and then she got busy with some other customers and was drawn away. As she did, John and I reflected on the conversation. What stood out to both of us was how she immediately negated my concerns and minimized any reasons that might call for more reflection. We commented on how there was just no talking to her, even if we had had several hours. She was on a mission, and there was no room for discussion. Not that she should have taken advice from a stranger, but it was the immediate dismissal of the concept that stood out.

> Due diligence is the practice of confirming that what you are getting is what you think you are getting.

At the same time, we could see something else. She did not have a clue about this guy. She couldn't have. She liked the package he was wrapped in, but her knowledge of what was inside was less than minimal. No one would even buy a carton of eggs without looking inside to see if they were okay, but she was willing to completely uproot her entire life, and the life of her young daughter as well, based on eight weeks of long-distance dating. Amazing. Really amazing. Not to mention the fact that the downside of waiting—i.e., having to change schools after a new semester begins—would be a whole lot easier than a failed marriage.

Yet this mistake happens every day. Instead of taking the time to see if the eggs are intact inside the carton of a relationship or a business deal, people like the way the outside looks, believe what they see, and jump right in. Often, to disastrous consequences.

Successful People Take Their Time

My server was about to make a very significant life decision in a very quick amount of time. In my experience, this is not what successful people do. But neither are they slow to act. So if quick is not good, and slow is not what successful people do, what in the world can we learn here?

In short, the answer is explained in a term you have heard in business, but one that applies to much more: "due diligence."

Said simply, in business, due diligence is the practice of confirming that what you are getting is what you think you are getting. Consider the words, "due," and "diligence." When something is due, it should be forthcoming *now*. It is *owed* to someone. It is a *right*, an *obligation*, a *fee*. And it is of a *proper quality*, such as "parenting with due care." When someone is diligent, they exert careful work or effort.

Put together, here is the principle:

> *I owe it to myself, and am obligated to myself, to pay* attention *in a* proper *way through a certain* necessary crucial time, *to carefully work to* find out if what I think I am getting is actually what I am getting.

And the reality of this is that whatever you are giving due diligence to can be done quickly or slowly, depending on two things: how good we are at seeing and how visible the reality is. Successful people know when they are good at seeing something, and they also know whether the reality can actually be seen. If either of these two are lacking, successful people do not move forward in anything of substance. They wait until they can see and until the reality can be seen. Said another way, "How is my vision?" and "How visible is the reality of what I am looking at?"

20/20 Vision: What You Need Determines What You See

When we want something to be true, we often see what we want to see. And at no time do we *want* something to be true more than when we *need* it to be true. Our need can truly color our judgment.

Our need can truly color our judgment.

When someone desperately needs a relationship or needs a business deal to go through or needs something else in life, they can color what they see and talk themselves into thinking, for example, that their shining knight on a white horse has shown up. They see what they want to see because they need it to be true.

Many years ago, one of the worst business decisions I ever made was to hire someone when I was in a state of need. I desperately needed someone to fill a position, and a person was referred to me with exactly the background and experience I needed in that job. In those ways, it was a perfect fit. Based on his past performance and experience, he had exactly the right qualifications.

At the same time, he was a bit odd. A nice guy, but somewhat wrapped up in himself and his accomplishments, and he was an incessant talker. Usually talking about himself.

Several people around me mentioned some of these traits and questioned what kind of team player he would be and how well he would fit in. In actuality, he was quite narcissistic, self-centered, socially clumsy, and thought "more highly of himself than he ought" (remember Romans 12:3?). But he came highly referred by someone others thought well of, so I overlooked what I saw and hired someone I turned into what I wanted to see.

The results were disastrous. He was not able to perform even close to the level I needed and expected, and it did not take long to see what I could not see earlier: This was a big mistake. And it cost me.

What was crazy, though, was that others around me could see what I was blinding myself to. And I am a professional! If this guy had walked into my office as a client, I would have seen things much more accurately. But the truth was that because I really needed to fill the position, I overlooked his narcissism and hired him for what I wanted him to be, not what he truly was. I learned a lesson that I will never forget: Just because I need someone to be something doesn't mean he is. I don't think I will make that mistake again.

But the phenomenon is true. Sometimes when we need something, we can make it look better than it actually is, and we omit data that might be staring us in the face. But due diligence would tell us that no matter how good something looks on the outside, it is only by taking a deeper, diligent, and honest look that we will find out what we truly need to know: the reality that we owe ourselves.

If I had taken the time to look further into this guy's background and circle of experiences and references, I would have seen the reality that was there. And I would have avoided joining his reality of non-performance. And I would not have had to pay for my mistake.

You have probably seen this dynamic lived out in relationships of someone you know. Maybe your friend is lonely or needy in some way, and she meets a person who seems to fulfill her dreams. She talks about this person in glowing terms, how "wonderful" he is. You are so happy for her and can't wait to meet Mr. Dreamboat.

Then you all have dinner together. And you are shocked: *Dreamboat is a nightmare.* The friends gather after dinner and all have the same question: *What is she thinking??*

The reality is that she isn't. She is idealizing someone out of her need for a relationship and the wish to see her guy as able to fill that need or void. It is clear to everyone except her that Dreamboat is going to sink soon, and it becomes public project number one to get her off that boat and into a lifeboat. But if you have ever tried to do that, you know that it's not easy. The need keeps her vision blurred, and you might even get barked at for trying to tell her what you see. And we have all had the experience of being avoided by people who did not want to hear what we were telling them.

So how will she see? *Due diligence*. Time and experience with the man of her dreams in a variety of contexts will show his true colors. Going through various seasons and experiences, as well as gaining other kinds of data will fill out the picture—if she will invest the time to do it. Seeing him interact with friends and family, observing his work and personal habits, his finances, spirituality, impulse control, stress tolerance, ability to delay gratification, etc., etc. All of this is part of diligently seeing the reality that she is due. If she will do it.

Another part of due diligence is gathering data from independent objective sources—from trusted friends with an unbiased viewpoint. Due diligence is the reason investors have an external audit done if they are thinking of buying a business. It is one thing to see a financial report that the owners put together. It is quite another to review an external audit. But we have to be willing to look and see.

I've had a lot of experience with boats, so a friend of mine—who wanted to get into boating—asked me to take a look at a vessel he was considering buying. It was a substantial purchase and a big commitment. A sixty-foot yacht requires a lot of work and attention. But when he told me about the yacht, it was clear that he was smitten. He loved the boat, and he loved the idea of being a boat owner.

I was excited to see it . . . until I did. I instantly saw several problems, not because I was smarter than he was, but because I have owned many boats *and I was objective.* I was not the one who wanted this boat, so I was able to look at it dispassionately and observe it for what it was: a lousy deal that would cause him problems and whose layout was not very usable, even though it was *attractive.* It was very impractical, and only an experienced boater would have known why.

When I went through the list of what was wrong with it, he was shocked. "I never would have thought of that," he said over and over. Why? He was in love. He had limited vision and was not objective. But we can all have 20/20 vision if we will ask experienced people we trust to take a look for us. We can borrow their eyes, unblurred by desire, ignorance, or prejudice.

If I buy something I do not know a lot about, like a house, I get a seasoned real estate friend to look at it for me. It is amazing what they see that I don't. Because of their experience and because they have no interest in buying it, they can see it for what it truly is. I have fallen in love with houses before, only to have my real estate agent or friend tell me why the house is a nightmare or a money pit. This is why you want a mechanic to look at a used car before you buy it: They know what they are looking for and have 20/20 vision, unaffected by either a lack of experience or being in love.

The Termite Reality: How Visible Is It?

Sometimes we think we have taken a good look at something, when in actuality there are things there that we can't see. I have some friends who recently went through the process of buying a home. They found one they loved and thought would be perfect for their family. It had a big yard and all the specific spaces they needed for all the ages. After several walk-throughs, visits, and bringing friends and family over, they decided to make an offer and put it under contract.

As part of the normal buying process, before the deal closes, there were multiple inspections to be done. Termites, soils and geological, electrical, plumbing, etc. These issues can be serious deal killers but are not visible to the naked eye upon an external viewing. It takes teams of professionals to look below the surface to see what is really going on in these areas. But the house looked to be in great shape, and they expected the inspections to run without a hitch.

> We can all have 20/20 vision if we will ask experienced people we trust to take a look for us.

Not so.

The geologist called them with bad news. "The retaining wall has some serious issues," he said. "I am e-mailing you a report, but you do not want to go forward without some serious concessions from the seller. This is going to be expensive to fix."

They were heartbroken, but also hoping that somehow he was wrong. His estimate for fixing the retaining wall was so expensive that it put the cost of the house over what they could afford. So they consulted another geologist.

The news was the same. The problem in the hillside was real, and if they did not fix it, it could slide and the house could come completely off the hillside and go into the stream below. So they called their agents and the sellers and began to negotiate.

At first the seller pushed back, saying this was just a false alarm, just an engineering opinion that he disagreed with, as he had lived there for a long time with no problem. But when my friends were willing to walk away from the deal if the wall was not fixed, the seller came around. Why? Reality had been duly, diligently discovered by two geologists, and there was no arguing or posturing anymore. It was what it was.

They negotiated a fair price for the fix, fixed the problem, and the deal went through. Now my friends are in the house safely, and all is fine. But what if they had gone through with the deal on the visible inspections they had made? They had 20/20 vision, but *all was not visible*. They had to look beneath the surface to what was not readily seen in order to get to the real facts.

Sometimes a hillside can be beautiful but have a soil problem under the retaining wall that can't be easily seen. It takes an expert inspection. Sometimes a house can look beautiful and yet have so many termites in the walls that the home is about to fall down. It takes an inspection to discover what is not visible.

The old saying "There's more than meets the eye" is true. A friend of mine told me that his daughter's boyfriend called and asked to take him to dinner. It went something like this:

"This can mean only one thing," he said. "He is going to ask for her hand in marriage. What in the world do I say? How do you handle this?"

"I know what I am going to say when that happens to me," I said.

"What?" he asked.

"I am going to tell him to come back with his credit report and his last two years' tax returns," I said.

He laughed out loud. "That's funny," he said, "but really, what will you say?"

"That really is what I will say. I am not kidding," I reiterated.

"You have got to be crazy," he said. "I don't care about how much money he makes. To ask would be offensive."

"I don't care about that, either," I said. "He can cross out the numbers if he wants. But I really do care about a couple of other things. First, does he have his tax returns? And is he current in paying his taxes, which shows responsibility.

"Second, what does his credit report show about other commitments he has made? Has he fulfilled covenants to other people and paid them what he said he would pay them? If he wants me to believe that he is going to fulfill the covenant he is making to my daughter, I want to see how faithful he has been in fulfilling promises he has made to people who are a much less valuable treasure than my daughter.

"Third, does he live within his means? Can he say no to his appetites when he can't afford them? Being a good husband means that he will sometimes have to sacrifice what he wants for a higher good. Can he do that? These are simple ways of getting a 'look-see' into his life and character," I said. "I am not kidding at all. Besides, I would not want her thinking things are fine while she is signing up for a world of problems and debt that she does not know about. Let's get it all out on the table."

"I never thought about it like that," he said. "I guess you really do have to look beneath the surface to find out what someone is really like."

He got it. None of these issues would have been visible by simply observing the nice-looking, clean-shaven, well-mannered young man who shows up every now and then at family functions. It takes a bit of an X-ray vision to see important qualities that are not visible to the naked eye.

Now, in other places where I have shared this story, I have gotten real pushback, such as "lots of good people have bad credit because they went through a hard time or illness. That is not fair," etc., etc. I understand and agree. But my questions are still good ones. And if there is a good reason for the bad credit— like an illness or layoff or even a past drug addiction that he has recovered well from—then fine. I got an answer. Then she knows what she is getting into, full disclosure, and I know what I am being asked to bless. I did not mean that the guy should have absolutely no issues to deal with—as when you buy a house with a leaky roof. These issues are not always deal breakers, but sometimes they are. I just want the truth. Then we can talk about what really is and possible wise solutions.

> It takes a bit of an X-ray vision to see important qualities that are not visible to the naked eye.

Ready, Aim, Fire

Due diligence is about keeping big decisions in the right order: *ready, aim, fire*. To do something right, we have to follow a process that ensures we are educated enough to make the decision or commitment, have good focus and knowledge of what we want, and are able to pull the trigger.

But sometimes we get the sequence wrong because we are too eager or too in love with an idea or person.

> *Instead of "ready, aim, fire," we go "fire, ready, aim."*

We pull the trigger before we have done the due diligence, and we get into trouble.

Ready

To be ready to make a good decision means that we know ourselves and our vulnerabilities. We know if we are too needy or vulnerable to make a good decision, or if we've done due diligence and are truly ready to look at our options and make a decision. We also know if we are strong enough to endure a mistake. How much will it hurt? Will it kill me? The wisest businesspeople I know sometimes pass on good deals or opportunities because they don't have the resources needed to proceed. They say, "That is a great opportunity, but we are just not ready for it. Our balance sheet is not where it needs to be," or "Our infrastructure is not ready and could not handle the growth that fast," or "My people are still two years away from being able to execute something that large." Or they say, "If this deal ran into any problems, our pockets are not deep enough to work them through." They wait until they are ready before they leap.

Aim

To aim means that we know that we have our goal and desire clearly in sight. Our focus is aligned with our mission and purpose. If we have not decided on the values we want to include in a relationship or business alliance, then anyone who comes along might do. But if we know that we want to share certain long-term values and purposes, then when someone good comes along but does not fit what we are aiming for in those key areas, we will pass—no matter how attractive the opportunity might be. We need to know what we are about, what we are looking for, and what we are focusing on in order for things to work well. Otherwise, we will be all over the map. Sometimes in business, an acquisition comes along that is a good deal but does not really fit the mission of the company, so they pass. Or perhaps a really good person comes along, but their values and priorities are not a match. So the company passes.

Fire

Finally, we have to be able to pull the trigger and go for it. We can never have 100 percent certainty. We have to take risks in order to grow and win. We cannot be impulsive, as we have been seeing, but neither can we be paralyzed, waiting to know things that are unknowable. After we are ready, and after we take aim to know our focus, we must be able to take the plunge.

How Long Before We *Know*?

That depends.

Researcher John Gottman can watch a couple interact for about fifteen minutes and tell you within a 90 percent accuracy whether they will be together or divorced after a certain period of time. It has been proven over and over. It seems as if he knows "instantly."

But he doesn't. His predictions are based on his *long-time due diligence*. He has spent thousands and thousands of hours dissecting and analyzing couple's interactions and has gotten his predictive system down to a science. He looks for four specific behaviors in each couple's interaction; if he sees them, he can know there's about a 90 percent chance the couple will not make it: defensiveness, contempt, criticism, and stonewalling.

Because of his thousands of hours in due diligence, he has the ability to see the truth in a matter of minutes. Doctors who have seen thousands of patients can diagnose some things in a few seconds. Their due diligence has built "pattern recognition" in their brains. Pattern recognition is the science of making inferences from perceptual data. *So the quick assessment of these experienced experts does not mean they are bypassing due diligence*. In fact, the opposite is true. They have been so diligent that drawing inferences is now a honed skill.

On the other hand, when business experts look at buying a business, their due diligence phase can take a long time. Even though they may have great pattern recognition, their accountants still need to get into the bowels of data—existing contracts, tax situations, market realities, etc. They need to see if what smells like a good deal actually is. Even experienced smart people sometimes require time to know what they don't know.

The principle is this: Do you really know what you *need* to know and what *can* be known? If you don't, beware of making a significant commitment, alliance, purchase, investment, or any other move that cannot easily be undone without a big cost. If you don't, it can cost you your heart, wallet, time, body, or even your life.

Due Diligence in Matters of the Heart

As we saw above, smart people will not make material investments without due diligence. The bank will not make you a loan without looking into your history with a fine-tooth comb. People do not buy houses without a termite inspection. Government agencies will not hire someone without a complete background check. A car dealer will not give you a serious, final price on a car without first running a credit check, and for sure would not give you the financing.

And all of these have to do with material purchases and

jobs. Yet in matters of the heart, which are much more serious, people give their hearts away every day without examining who they are giving them to. It would seem that we would be more careful with our hearts, minds, and souls than with our money or careers, as important as they are. But we aren't.

God has said in many ways to be diligent and careful. Proverbs 21:5 says: "The plans of the diligent lead to profit as surely as haste leads to poverty" (NIV). As we have seen, when we are hasty, we can lose everything. And when we don't carefully consider all of the factors, things can end very badly:

> *Suppose one of you wants to build a tower. Won't*
> *you first sit down and estimate the cost to see if*
> *you have enough money to complete it? For if*
> *you lay the foundation and are not able to finish*
> *it, everyone who sees it will ridicule you, saying,*
> *"This person began to build and wasn't able to finish."*
> *Or suppose a king is about to go to war against another*
> *king. Won't he first sit down and consider whether*
> *he is able with ten thousand men to oppose the one*
> *coming against him with twenty thousand? If he is*
> *not able, he will send a delegation while the other is*
> *still a long way off and will ask for terms of peace.*
> *—Luke 14:28–32, NIV*

If we choose people for significant positions in life without being diligent, we might share in their problems and inflict ourselves: Don't be too quick to appoint anyone as an elder, and don't share in the sins of others. Keep yourself pure (1 Timothy 5:22, HCSB).

The behavior that successful people never go back to is *making decisions without first knowing what they are getting themselves into.* Usually, they have had an experience or two to teach them that not doing due diligence can really, really cost— in heart, mind, soul, strength, as well as in time and treasure. Take your time.

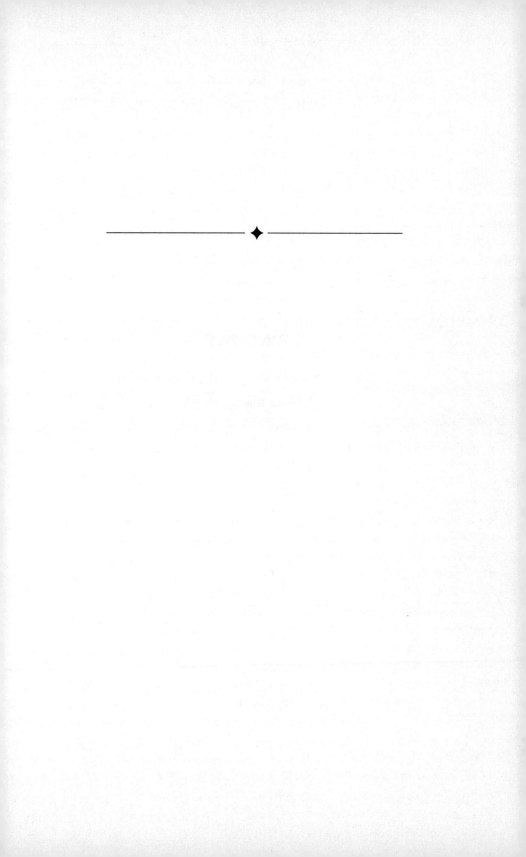

Let us examine our ways and test them.
—Lamentations 3:40a, NIV

PRINCIPLE

**Never go back to ignoring the part you play
in being where you are.**

—

CHAPTER 9

NEVER AGAIN . . .

FAIL TO ASK WHY YOU ARE WHERE YOU ARE

I was leading a group one day when a woman exclaimed, "Okay! I get it! I have had nine abusive husbands, and I am not going to get another one!"

Another woman spoke up and said, "No you haven't. You've had one abusive husband with nine different names. You always pick the same man, over and over again."

Ouch. Sometimes the truth hurts. In all of these marriages, she was the common denominator. She was able to find a certain type, with certain behaviors, and choose that man above all others. The lesson: *She was playing a part in where she was.*

One of the biggest differences between successful people and others is that in love and in life, in relationships and in business, successful people always ask themselves, *what part am I playing in this situation?* Said another way, they do not see themselves only as victims, even when they are. They also ask if there is something to be learned about themselves so they can either turn the situation around or make sure they never find themselves in it ever again. They say something like this: "I have contributed to this in some way. What do I need to learn?"

These people realize that wherever we find ourselves in life, we are not only acted *upon*, but we are also *actors*. We play a part in where we are, and when we learn what that part is and what we are contributing to being there, new doors and new paths begin to open up.

I was doing a seminar one day when a woman asked this question: "How do you deal with critical people?"

My first response was, "Why would you want to do that? Dealing with critical people is awful."

She looked at me like I was crazy and said, "Well . . . because you have to!"

"I don't find that to be true," I said. "Why do you *have to*?"

She got very circumspect and almost in a whisper so no one could hear, she said, "Because they're *everywhere*!"

"Everywhere?" I asked.

"Yes. Everywhere," she said.

"Wow. Let's talk about that."

And we did, right there in front of a thousand people. I asked her what these critical people were like and where she was finding them, and she began to describe judgmental, critical personalities that she knew in her work, her church, her extended family, her social circles, and pretty much everywhere she was involved. In a sense, she was right. They were everywhere—at least in *her everywhere*. Apparently, she had an uncanny ability to find them, no matter where she was.

It seemed that at her company or in church or pretty much

any other circle, she would somehow manage to be drawn to the most critical person in the group and become friends with them. Then after a while, she would feel like "all they do is criticize what I am doing and tell me I should be doing it differently."

What she had never thought about was that she had a strong tendency to feel bad when someone was critical of her and a strong drive to then gain their approval. So when a critical personality was somewhere in the mix, she was drawn to that person more than to others because she felt driven to make him like her.

What I told her was that while it was true that critical people can be found everywhere, it was not true that she had to keep finding them or become best friends with them. But as long as she needed the approval of critical people—which is impossible to attain—she would always need to find a critical person so that she could live out her lifelong strategy of finally getting one to like her. Good luck.

> While it was true that critical people can be found everywhere, it was not true that she had to keep finding them.

The observation here is that *she needed a critical person to accomplish her goal of getting critical people to finally approve of her. Her "script" required a critical person, so without realizing it, she always looked for one.* All she would know was that when she encountered a critical person, she would feel "not good enough" and would begin trying to be good enough in their eyes, exerting lots of effort and continually falling short.

"So, what do I do?" she said.

"Easy," I said. "Just be honest with them and you will never hear from them again."

"What?" she said.

"Just be honest with them," I said. "Tell them, something like, 'Yeah, I can see that you would do it differently, but I like it like this. What's for lunch?'"

"But they will keep telling me what is wrong with what I am doing."

"Probably. So then you just say, 'Yeah, I understand you feel that way, but that is the way I want to do it. Let's move on. What's for lunch?'"

I could see in her face that to just leave it at that was going to be a big growth step for her, and I knew the reason. If she changed her reaction, she would have to give up her wish for critical people to turn into approving people. She would have to wave the white flag and give up on her lifelong strategy to change critical people's minds and just accept them as who they are: Dogs bark, and critical people criticize. That's what they do until they change. Your being good enough is not going to change them into being noncritical any more than it could make a dog start meowing.

Her lesson was to ask the question that this chapter asks: What role am I playing in the situation that I find myself? What am I contributing to this? For one thing, she was enabling them to hold that position in her life.

But up until she asked herself that question, she had seen the world as full of critical people whom she desired to turn into noncritical people. But if she asks the question "Why do I keep finding these people and getting into this powerful dynamic with them?" she'll come up with something *actionable*.

She'll understand that she has a driving need to change their minds, to finally win them over, to make them like her. She'll understand that their criticism bothers her and that it has the power to make her feel bad. And since she didn't like feeling bad, she felt compelled to do something in order to feel good. Her something was to try to win them over. "Win them over, then they will like me, then I will feel good."

Understanding all this gives her something she can actually work on. She can work on her tendency to allow critical people to have that kind of power over her. She can work on staying separate from their opinions of her and have her own. And most powerfully, she can finally notice that there are other people in the room (of life) who are not critical, and she can begin to allow them to matter to her more than the critical people. She can then accept their acceptance, thereby reducing the power of the critical ones.

These realizations about herself—not just about the other person—give her something to work on that she actually has control over: *herself*. And when we begin to change, then the situations we find ourselves in begin to change as well. That is the essence of this principle.

The Bible describes this dynamic:

> *Above all else, guard your heart,*
> *for everything you do flows from it.*
> *—Proverbs 4:23, NIV*

What the Bible teaches, and what all psychological research validates, is that we play a part in our life situations. Our appetites, our needs, our views of life, our biases, our tastes, our hurts, fears, issues, and backgrounds—all play a role in what we do. Who we are on the inside plays a role in many situations in which we find ourselves.

The woman we talked about above had a need in her heart to get approval from critical people. And this drive manifested itself in her seeing the world as composed of critical people who made her life miserable. She had to learn that if she would work on what was inside of her, these people would largely disappear from her radar. If she could change, her life situations would change.

The Issue of Codependency

In the last several decades of addiction treatment, one of the most powerful discoveries has been the role of the codependent in addictions. Basically, researchers learned that an addict needs a codependent to enable staying addicted. But beyond that, codependent people continually find themselves in relationships with addicts. In my experience with codependents, I've often heard, "Out of all the people in the world, I will be drawn to the addict before anyone else."

One reason for this attraction is that there is a *match*. The addict does not take responsibility for his life, and the codependent feels responsible to take care of people who are not taking responsibility for themselves. So the addict and the codependent will be drawn to people who fill their needs. And it works . . . for a while . . . until . . .

When the codependent finally asks the question of this chapter—"What is it about me that always draws me into this kind of relationships?"—then she learns what codependency is and begins to work on it. Once she gets further down that path and changes those patterns, her whole world begins to look different. It is no longer filled with addicts, but with loving and responsible people. Voilà!! She changed, and the world changed.

Even when a situation is someone else's fault, we sometimes play a part in it. At the very least, we may be failing to confront an individual and set boundaries. When that happens, we enable the problem to continue, and we must ask ourselves, *what is my part in this?*

> Who we are on the inside plays a role in many situations in which we find ourselves.

When I was trained in addictions treatment, I was taught that the codependent plays a role in the addiction of the person they are connected to; and when I began to interact with clients, I was amazed at how true that was. Change the codependent, and the addict often changes as well. I was pretty impressed with the wisdom of the addiction specialists when I was a grad student.

But then, I was even more impressed when I learned that these specialists were not the first to speak of this principle. God was. Listen to this passage from Leviticus:

Do not hate a fellow Israelite in your heart.
Rebuke your neighbor frankly
so you will not share in their guilt.
—Leviticus 19:17, NIV

The Bible tells us that when someone needs to be confronted, we are to confront them and set limits with them, or we will "share in their guilt." In other words, we are part of the problem if we are enabling it and are being codependent.

When we understand our part in a negative situation and do what we need to do, we can change the situation—or at least change ourselves.

Whatever negative issues we are facing, change begins when we ask ourselves, *what inside of me needs to change for this to get better?*

Results Talk to Us

I love to listen to people explain why they are where they are in life. People are amazing, and I love to see how they navigate life and use their talents and skills. I see so many beautiful portraits of love and accomplishments in people's stories.

> Some people live their lives, while others allow their lives to live them.

But as I listen, I also find that there are two types of people in these stories. Some people live their lives, while way too many others allow their lives to live them. These people live life as if they are along for the ride and life is something that just happens to them. They do not see their part in what is happening.

I had a friend—we'll call him Jay—who was experiencing a pattern that he did not recognize as *his* pattern. He saw it as a string of companies that did not recognize his talents and his value and sold him short. In three different situations, he had big VP roles and was very successful. Jay was a good performer in certain areas and was a natural for becoming the CEO in any of these companies. But each time, his own boss—the current CEO—would recommend someone else when it came time for the decision. Disappointed and feeling cheated out of what he deserved, Jay would leave the company and be picked up by one who saw him as a great candidate. Then it would happen again.

Recently, I had dinner with a friend who had worked with Jay in one of those companies; it happened to be a company where I had also done business. Jay's name came up, and we began to reflect on all the great experiences and times we had had with him, as well as on the big issue of his being passed up for CEO, even though it had appeared that he was the obvious choice. In passing, I commented, "One thing about Jay that made working with him less than ideal was that he didn't really listen. I found that I could not get him to hear my concerns or understand that I needed the company to change certain things. He would always find a way to negate my concern and not hear it."

My friend looked at me and said, "You know . . . I never put it together like that, but I always felt a cringe in my gut when

I thought about him becoming the CEO. I knew he was great, but whenever he was mentioned as the future CEO—and as my boss—I had an uneasy feeling, even as great as he was. In a subtle way, you never could tell him anything."

It all became clear why this well-connected, incredibly talented, experienced, and brilliant guy would continually get passed over for a position that he was absolutely capable of performing. He was not a victim of unfair bosses or companies who did not recognize his value. Instead, he was passed over because he created an uneasy feeling in other people that he could not listen to or adapt to input. Consciously or unconsciously, bosses and boards felt that and could not put him in charge.

What if after the first time of being passed up—or even before that—he had thought, *I wonder what part I play in not getting this promotion? I am going to ask people if there is anything they see that I should work on.* He could have worked on his listening skills and probably would have become a CEO along the way, and his lifelong path would have culminated in a position commensurate with his talents. Instead, something about his makeup got in the way of his talents realizing their full potential.

The lesson? He was not a victim of bad companies, even though some people are. His problem was that he failed to ask the all-important questions: Why am I here again? What role am I playing in this situation? What do I need to change to make the next one different, or even this one? What am I contributing to this dynamic?

God's Wisdom on the Matter

Again, God tells us to never go back to seeing ourselves only as victims of every situation:

Consider it pure joy, my brothers and sisters,
whenever you face trials of many kinds,
because you know that the testing of your faith
produces perseverance.
Let perseverance finish its work
so that you may be mature and complete,
not lacking anything.
If any of you lacks wisdom,
you should ask God,
who gives generously to all without finding fault,
and it will be given to you.
—James 1:2–5, NIV

In a sense, this entire awakening or realization, this entire "repentance" is summed up in this passage. It is the need to "never go back" to seeing ourselves only as a "poor me victim in a bad situation," but to ask ourselves, *What do I need to learn from this, and how can this situation be used to make me more "complete," so I am not lacking in anything? How can I use it to be wiser and not allow people to do this again, or not repeat the mistakes that are causing this pattern?* The above James passage teaches us three things:

1. It Starts with Attitude: Consider It Joy When You Face Trials

What, God? Are you kidding me? I just got passed over for CEO after working my butt off for years, and you want me to be joyful about it? Are you crazy?

That would be a normal response. Getting passed over for a promotion or being in a relationship with an addict or being abandoned in a divorce is not a joyful experience.

But God is not telling us not to feel the pain, hurt, and disappointment in these trials. He is saying something different. Feel the pain, but take a different stance toward the situation. See it as a situation where you can learn and be made complete. Where you can get better. This is not the kind of testing where you get a passing or failing grade. The word used in this passage refers to testing certain metals in order to remove the impurities so that they become stronger and better.

Our tough situations can be used, if we choose, to remove our weaknesses and patterns that are currently getting in the way of the life God has created us for. They can teach us and make us better and healthier. I have heard many great performers tell me that losing a particular job or a particular deal was the best thing that ever happened to them, because it showed them an area where they needed to get better. After they got better, they were able to accomplish their goals. Which brings us to the second point we learn from the passage above:

2. Trials Produce Maturity, so That We Are Not Lacking in Anything

If we bail out or quit when we are in a difficult situation and simply see ourselves as victims, we never learn. In the James passage, God tells us to face the trial and look for how it is testing us, so that we can become complete and learn what we need to learn. Once we do, we can move on to better things.

My twelve-year-old daughter, Olivia, and I were studying this passage just this morning, as I told her I was writing on it. I asked her for her thoughts about it and to give me a situation that she could apply it to. She told me she is participating in a particular sport that she has not played before and is not very good at. As a result, she is not put in the game much and is riding the bench. She has been discouraged about it; in her other sports, she is a superstar and doesn't spend much time on the bench. I asked her what this passage said to her, and this is what she said:

"I guess I have been wanting to quit, and I've been feeling like I am not good enough. But what the passage says is that I need to think a different way," she said.

"How is that?" I asked.

"Well . . . I need to just play. Not quit, but just play and get better. Then I will get into the game," she said. "If I stick to it, I will get better and then I will get to play."

I high-fived her. She got it. She was growing in maturity. Just last week at dinner she was dejected about not getting much play time; this week, as a result of this passage, I expect that I will see a different kid. She will stick to it; she'll persevere, as the passage says, with the view that "this situation can teach me something. I have to keep going and learn its lesson." And she will.

But to me, as her dad, what I am much more excited about than her getting better at volleyball is that she has grown one step closer to learning this principle: when things are hard, get an attitude of joy and persevere to learn what you need to learn. Then, you will not lack that skill any more.

But how? The passage tells us. Help comes from the outside.

3. It Ends with God's Love: Not Finding Fault

One of my favorite, favorite phrases in this entire passage is the phrase "without finding fault." Read the passage again:

> *Consider it pure joy, my brothers and sisters,*
> *whenever you face trials of many kinds,*
> *because you know that the testing of your faith*
> *produces perseverance.*
> *Let perseverance finish its work*
> *so that you may be mature and complete,*
> *not lacking anything.*
> *If any of you lacks wisdom, you should ask God,*
> *who gives generously to all* without finding fault,
> *and it will be given to you.*
> —James 1:2–5, NIV

One of our biggest problems is that when we do not know how to do something or when we fail at something, we see ourselves in a critical light. We start thinking that we're not good enough and, therefore, are "bad," or "less than." But this passage says that God does not look at us in a critical fashion, "finding fault." He is not up there going, "You idiot! If you weren't like this or that, you could do it. You are a loser and here is why!" He is not "finding fault" with us—what an encouraging truth!

Instead, he wants to help us learn what we need to learn in order to become "complete" in our abilities. He understands that we need some wisdom, some maturity, in order to do it right. And notice what it says about how he approaches us? *Generously.* Not critical of our faults, but generous to give us the wisdom we need to do it better, to be made complete.

The next time you feel like you ought to be doing better in a particular situation and are "finding fault" with yourself, take the same attitude toward yourself that God has toward you: believe him when he says it is not about finding fault; it is about learning. And even if you are stuck and don't know what to do—remember, all you have to do is ask God for wisdom and he will give it to you *generously.* He will be gracious and give you the help and guidance you need.

The Great Paradox

Some of the greatest truths of the Judeo-Christian faith are powerful paradoxes—a tension of two, seemingly opposite truths that exist side by side in perfect balance. The passage we looked at in James contains one of those perfectly balanced paradoxes—two truths existing in life-shaping tension. In James, God says we *do* have a responsibility to grow and change regarding the problems we face. But he also says he does not shame or condemn us for our need to grow. In principle, he says, "Do better. Grow. Mature." While at the same time, he says, "I am not on your case about your lack of maturity; I am not finding fault. I will give you wisdom to get through this." As the psalmist says,

> *As a father has compassion on his children,*
> *so the LORD has compassion on those who fear him;*
> *for he knows how we are formed, he remembers*
> *that we are dust.*
> —*Psalm 103:13–14, NIV*

God knows that we need to grow and get better, and at the same time, he accepts us as we are. This truth helps us break through one of the biggest barriers to learning the lesson of this chapter. It is hard for us to take responsibility for where we need to change, because we feel "bad" for not being good enough. We feel ashamed and guilty. And because we feel bad, we don't look at ourselves. Instead, we feel victimized by the "bad boss" or the "addict who is making my life miserable" or whomever is on the other side of our struggle.

And the truth is that many times we are right—other people cause us problems. An addict who is making your life miserable truly is at fault. The boss who is not helping you truly is at fault. The critical person who is being mean and critical truly is at fault. So, blaming is easy and often right, because others are often at fault.

But when we look only at the trouble the other person is

causing, we fail to ask, *what do I need to change in order to change things?* If we simply blame the other person, we miss the "completing" that the situation offers us. Even if they are at fault, we can still learn. If we only look at them, we miss what we need to learn, so we will probably find ourselves in the same situation again, dealing with one more critical person we try to get approval from. Or one more addict we try to cure. Or one more mean coach who won't let us in the game. And on and on.

But, when we accept God's grace and help, we can do two things: We can forgive the other person for their wrong if needed, and we can look in the mirror and see where we need to grow and what part we are playing in the situation.

Not New Age

Before we move on, I want to make clear what I am *not saying and what the Bible never says.*

I am not saying that all your struggles are in some way your fault. That is not true. Bad people happen to good people. Every day. Some people are true victims of mistreatment, abuse, crime, abandonment, etc. And sometimes something horrible happens to you that you played no role in whatsoever. The Bible affirms the innocent and that people are innocently harmed by bad people. And it also says that God is on your side and will help you when that happens. (See passages such as Proverbs 18:5; Isaiah 29:20–22; and Amos 5:12.)

So do not take this lesson to mean that you somehow cause all of the bad things that happen to you. That is just not true.

But many people, both Christian and not, sometimes imply that we *do* cause any bad thing that happens to us, or that God is punishing us for something, or other weird thinking. New Age thinking has a lot of this in it. It says that whatever you experience, you somehow "attracted" to yourself through your thoughts or behavior—good or bad.

In 2008, I lost three people in a period of a few months. Both of my parents died, one right after the other; and then my brother-in-law, Mark, a Navy SEAL, was killed in Iraq. It was one of the most difficult times I have ever been through. It was one death right after another, and it was too much to process.

A few months later, I got a call from a media person I sometimes work with, and he asked how I was doing. I told him, "Not so well," and explained that I had just gone through three deaths of people very close to me. As a New Ager who believes that everything comes from the Law of Attraction, he said, "You had better figure out how you are attracting so much death into your life and deal with it."

I was stunned. I was not really hurt by his words, as I did not know him well enough for him to hurt me. But I was shocked that someone would actually believe that and that he would say it to someone in grief. Amazing . . . like I caused their deaths in some way.

But in my experience, I've talked with many who have been blamed by others for the atrocities that happened to them—as if they were somehow asking for it. Do not blame yourself for bad things that happen to you or for the bad treatment that others inflict on you. God affirms that some people truly are innocent victims who are mistreated at the hands of other people. Do not blame yourself for their actions when you have been victimized.

God Will Rescue

The overwhelming biblical theme in situations of oppression is that God will rescue the oppressed. If you find yourself being victimized, reach out to God and reach out to others for help. And even though you are not causing the abuse, you can ask yourself what steps you need to take to get out of it. Who do you need to call? What skills do you need to develop? Who do you need to ask to protect you? Then reach out. Listen to the promises of God:

> *The righteous cry out, and the LORD hears them;*
> *he delivers them from all their troubles.*
> *The LORD is close to the brokenhearted*
> *and saves those who are crushed in spirit.*
> *—Psalm 34:17–18, NIV*

If there is little you can do to affect a person or a situation, there is one thing you can always do: reach out for help—to God and to others. He will come to your aid.

An Empowering Message of Hope

One of the most difficult feelings in life is the feeling of powerlessness. Helplessness. We often experience it in situations where something or someone outside of our control affects our well-being. We begin to personalize the situation, thinking it is hopeless.

The great thing about this lesson of the Bible and its never-go-back effects is that even when we find ourselves in negative situations or destructive patterns, we are not powerless victims. We can learn from the situation. We can learn how to deal differently with a person or institution. We can learn not to allow someone else to have power over us and affect us negatively. We can sometimes learn how we may be contributing to the pattern through enabling, choices, or lack of skills. And we can always ask God for help.

That is a powerful awakening. No matter where we find ourselves, God has something for us to learn and can bring good out of even the most painful situations.

The fruit of the righteous is a tree of life.
—*Proverbs 11:30a, NIV*

PRINCIPLE

Never go back to forgetting that life is lived inside out.

CHAPTER 10

NEVER AGAIN . . .

FORGET THAT YOUR INNER LIFE DETERMINES YOUR OUTER SUCCESS

My client was a very successful president of a technology company. He had led his company to incredible growth and profits and was a bit of a star in his industry. At forty, his future looked bright—very bright.

But then something happened to change all of that, at least in his mind. His company was being bought by a Japanese firm, and as he looked at the chessboard, he knew it could only mean one thing for him—he was going to be let go. His particular product space was redundant—the new company already had that area covered. He was certain the new company would fold his division into their existing one, and he would no longer be needed. He was sure they would keep their own president in place.

It was interesting to watch what happened. He had just begun with me in executive coaching, so I had been working with him only about six months. But I had enough experience with him to know he was very, very sharp. He was smart, creative, and innovative, great with people and with the business side of technology. He had come from a technology background, but when he got a taste of the business side of it all in his early thirties, he had never looked back. And he had done very well, making a well-known name for himself in the industry.

Which made his reaction to this development all the more surprising. When he first told me he would probably be let go, I was actually excited for him! My first thought was that with all he had accomplished and all of his brains and talents, companies all over the world would be standing in line to hire him. He was going to win the lottery. Or, potentially even more exciting, he would be a prime target for an investment bank to fund for a new acquisition that he could head up or for a new venture altogether. The future looked incredible from my viewpoint. He was a shoo-in for a CEO role somewhere good.

But from his viewpoint, he did not see any of that. *He just saw his job disappearing*. He saw the company he had built going away and changing. He saw his career ending, not knowing what in the world, if anything, would be next. I was surprised when he called me in a worried state.

"I can't sleep," he said. "I find myself lying there wondering what is going to happen."

"When you do that, what do you imagine?" I asked.

"I keep having these pictures of me being in some job that I hate, probably in the middle of nowhere, not making any money and not having any future. I feel like I'll end up almost homeless or something. I know it sounds kind of crazy, but that is what I keep thinking," he explained. "I feel like it's over."

That *was* crazy, at least in any real sense of what would likely happen. From where I sat, he could and would pretty much write his own ticket. The opportunities would be enormous. But he could not see that. So I asked him a question: "So . . . where do you think this last job came from?"

"It came from my last boss who moved from the previous company. He took me with him, and I got promoted when he retired. But he is gone now, and I won't be getting any help from him."

"And where do you think that came from?" I asked.

"What? My boss? From the old company," he reiterated.

"No, not your boss. Where did your boss *wanting to hire you* come from?" I pressed.

"He liked me and thought I could fit well in the new business," he said.

"And why did he think that?"

At this point, he knew I was after something, so he just asked, "So what are you trying to say?"

"I am not trying to say anything," I said. "I am trying to get you to say something. I am trying to get you to see where your career *came* from. Where your current job, previous job, or any other job *came* from for that matter. I am trying to get you to see where your performance *came* from."

"Why?" he said. "I don't get it."

"Because if you could see where it came from, you would know that it has not gone away."

"What?" he asked. "I don't get it. It has gone away."

> From where I sat, he could pretty much write his own ticket.

"No it hasn't," I said. "And that is my point."

"Meaning?"

"Meaning, you keep looking at your job or your boss or certain circumstances as being on the *outside*, and you think the source of what you have is outside of you. You think that this boss or this company was where your job and career came from; you think you are just lucky. But that is not true," I explained.

"Still not getting it," he said. "They *were* where they came from. I didn't imagine those people and the company. I have worked there for a long time."

"I know. But *they hired you for a reason that had nothing to do with them.*" They hired you for reasons that had to do with you, and those reasons have not gone away."

"Keep going. . . ." he said.

"You keep thinking that all of this stuff—your job, your career, your boss—is where your reality came from; and now that they have gone away, you think you have "lost it all." But that is not true.

"What is true is that you are not seeing where it all *came* from. Your success came from God and from inside *you*— what God put *inside* you, how he *gifted* you, the opportunities he put in front of you, and what you have developed: *your heart, your mind, your soul, your strength, your talents, your energy*—all of which is still there. You took all of that to the outside world and invested it in life, and you

> "Your success came from God and from inside *you*—what God put *inside* you, how he *gifted* you, and what you have developed."

reaped the results of investing who *you* are and investing in who God is. You invested the *invisible* you, the inside you—your talents, brains, energy, heart, all of it. That is where your 'career' came from, and you have lost *none* of that. God has not gone away, and your insides have not gone away either. Even though the 'outside' job is gone, where it came from still remains.

"So you still have everything that created what you think you have lost. In reality, you have lost nothing. It is like when a hen loses an egg: she doesn't get scared. She knows she can make another one.

"You are scared because you don't see the true reality. *There is only one reality, and it works like this*: God gives you talents, heart, brain, abilities, energy, a mind, a soul, and time to invest them. And he gives you a context within which to invest them. Your investment of all that heart and strength determines your path. And God directs your steps, bringing you the opportunities, doors to walk through, people to meet, etc. The *invisible you: your heart, mind, soul, and strength, is where it all came from—with God's help. And all of that is still there, stronger than ever*. If you would realize that, you would realize that you have lost nothing and that you can re-create all of it because you still have all of that ability, and God is still in your life," I said.

"Honestly, I have never thought about it that way. If I did it once, I can probably do it again. Is that what you are saying?"

"Pretty much," I said, "plus the fact that God is still there and is always invested in our growth and development. So the fact is that you probably won't just do it again. You will do it *better* than the last time. You will probably do *more*, because you are further developed and ready for more. You have lost nothing of who you are and are ready to pick up even more weight, more challenge, more growth. As God says, 'He who is faithful in little, will be given more.' You just watch. I dare you." I was sure, and I was hoping he could be sure as well.

I then asked him to make a list of his talents, abilities, networks, relationships, experiences, strengths, etc., and bring them in to me when he came for his next visit. When he looked at the list, he realized he was carrying around a lot of ability and that his ability—catalyzed by his investment of time and energy and by God's leading—truly was where his career had come from. As he saw this, his view of life began to change. He began to see one of the most important awakenings we can ever have:

Our life is never on the outside.
It is always on the inside.
The invisible life always produces the visible life.
Life works "inside out."

The Reality of "The Good Life"

In the chapter about *why you are where you are*, we saw that our own issues often contribute in a negative way to the challenges we find ourselves in. We saw how important it is to look at ourselves and make the changes needed to grow through trials and difficulties so we can become more complete. And we've spent much of the book exploring those needed changes.

In this chapter, we take that concept to the next level by

looking at the *positive* contributions we make to our life situations. When we understand that good lives are not found or lost only due to circumstances, we learn to contribute to the production of "the good life" all around us, no matter what situation we find ourselves in. We find that two things are true: First, the good life sometimes has little to do with outside circumstances. We are happy and fulfilled mostly by who we are on the inside. Research validates that. Second, our internal lives largely contribute to producing many of our external circumstances—in a good sense. Our talents and abilities, when invested with God, actually build much of the external life. When we invest our talents, there is fruit. Let's look at both of those.

1. The Good Life Is Not on the Outside

Both the Bible and scientific research reveal that our outside circumstances have very little to do with our well-being. In *The Law of Happiness*, I wrote about the scientific research on happiness. For the past several years, the scientific community has done massive research on happiness, well-being, and thriving. Scientists began to ask, What makes people happy? When people are happy, what causes it? And they have found some very robust answers—answers that surprise us because they don't conform with the way we naturally think. Actually, the findings are the opposite of how we naturally think. Here is a summary of the research findings on happiness:

Only 10 percent of our happiness comes from the circumstantial, or external. Our thinking often goes like this: "If I just had more money, or that particular job, or that relationship, or that house, or were married, or were single, or lived in that neighborhood, or could retire, or, or, or, or—*then I would be happy.*" But research reveals that circumstances contribute only about 10 percent to our happiness and well-being! When we do have some change in circumstances, we get a "bump" of only around 10 percent, and then go right back to our "set point" of *who we are as a person.* Said another way,

> *We are who we are;*
> *outside circumstances do not*
> *change who we are on the inside.*

For example, if someone is an unhappy single person and they get married, they will probably be an unhappy married person—even if they thought that marriage would make them happy. The same is true of landing a particular job or achieving any other accomplishment. You get a temporary 10 percent bump in happiness, and then the new-car smell goes away. Or as one woman said, "The new-husband smell goes away." The honeymoon ends, and you are still you.

The remaining 90 percent of happiness comes from two places. The first chunk comes from your basic temperament, constitutional makeup, etc. It is a combination of biology and a bunch of other developmental realities. Go into a nursery and observe the newborns; you will see that some of them are already smiling and happy with the world, and others are not so happy. Babies are born with a tendency toward happiness or unhappiness—but that tendency amounts to only part of their future happiness.

The rest of your happiness comes *not* from circumstances or biology, but from a set of life practices, attitudes, and behaviors. In other words, *much of your happiness comes from who you choose to develop on the inside. The real you. The spiritual you that God has created and that you are choosing to develop.*

The scientific research affirms what God tells us over and over again: If we pay attention to the inside of us, the *invisible* us, then the outside will take care of itself.

> Your happiness comes from who you choose to develop on the inside.

Every good tree bears good fruit,
but a bad tree bears bad fruit.
A good tree cannot bear bad fruit,
and a bad tree cannot bear good fruit.
—*Matthew 7:17–18, NIV*

While circumstances play a role (10 percent), so much of happiness comes from "the tree," or said in the terms of this chapter, "our insides." To the degree that we are developing the tree, "our insides," we will bear fruit, beginning with the fruit of "being happy." Developing our tree, our internal life and character, will produce the good fruits of relationships, talents, growing finances, and much more. In order to have the outside life we desire, we must seek God and develop as people. As Jesus said,

This is why I tell you: Don't worry about your life,
what you will eat or what you will drink; or about your

body, what you will wear. Isn't life more than food
and the body more than clothing? Look at the birds
of the sky: They don't sow or reap or gather into barns,
yet your heavenly Father feeds them. Aren't you
worth more than they? Can any of you add a single
cubit to his height by worrying? And why do you worry
about clothes? Learn how the wildflowers of the field
grow: they don't labor or spin thread. Yet I tell you
that not even Solomon in all his splendor was adorned
like one of these! If that's how God clothes the grass
of the field, which is here today and thrown into the
furnace tomorrow, won't He do much more for you—you
of little faith? So don't worry, saying, 'What will we eat?'
or 'What will we drink?' or 'What will we wear?' For the
idolaters eagerly seek all these things, and your heavenly
Father knows that you need them. But seek first the
kingdom of God and His righteousness, and all these
things will be provided for you. *Therefore don't worry*
about tomorrow, because tomorrow will worry about
itself. Each day has enough trouble of its own.
—*Matthew 6:25–34, HCSB*

2. The Good Life Comes from the Inside

Our true life doesn't consist of the outside. It consists of our spiritual life—seeking God and his righteousness and his ways. When we do that, he promises that the outside will take care of itself.

The implications of putting spiritual growth and health first are as big as life itself:

*Spiritual health gives us direction and helps us
prioritize our lives.*

Spiritual growth becomes a compass, a True North. If we know that the most important thing in life is our internal life, then we will choose to devote time and energy to seeking God and our spiritual development before we seek anything else. We will seek the increasing growth and capacities of our heart, mind, soul, and strength. If we really, really believe that is where life comes from, then we will do everything to make sure our "tree" is healthy and strong before we expect the tree to develop fruit.

Developing our inner selves first helps us prioritize our lives. We know that our first order of business is to tend our inner tree. Remember the earlier proverb, "Guard your heart with all diligence, for from it flow the issues of life"? This is what that means. When we look to our inner selves, we begin to be a guardian of our hearts, making sure that they are strong and healthy, because we know that the fruitfulness of our lives will come from our hearts. Our hearts will determine the "issues" of our lives.

The fruitfulness of our lives will come from our hearts.

We all have a lot of "issues" in life. We may have dysfunctional relationships, floundering careers, burnout, stress, lost dreams, debt, and more. But the truth is that many of those issues come as a result of whether or not we are tending to and guarding our "inside life," our heart, mind, soul, and strength.

But we don't have only bad "issues"; we can have good

issues, too! If our hearts are healthy, our lives will reflect that health in the kinds of "issues" we have.

What if—as a result of growing, getting healthy, and becoming involved and invested—you were able to say things like . . .

- I have so many great relationships that I have to figure out how to find the time for all of them!

- My career is going so well, I have a hard time figuring which of the opportunities to decide upon. There are too many!

- I have so many things I am burning to do and only one life to do them in!

- I feel so much connection to God, even in bad circumstances, that there is not enough time to tell everyone I know about how good He is!

- Every dream that gets realized births five more! Life has so much to offer that I need some coaching to figure out the best from the good.

- I need to find some good places to give my "overflow" money.

You get the idea, and there are many people, just like you, who have to deal with those positive "issues" every day. As you get healthier and healthier, you will, too.

So, the good news is this: when the Bible says that our insides— our hearts in particular—determine the issues of life, it does not only mean "negative issues," but *all* issues. Think of the issues a lonely person has versus the issues a person with a large circle of friends has. They have different issues, but often those issues stem from the health of their relational world, which in turn comes from their internal lives—like how trusting they allow themselves to be or how assertive they are or how they deal with conflict or their willingness to forgive or whether they put themselves out there, take risks, and keep going when it gets painful. We each play a big role in what the "issues of our lives" turn out to be.

This does not mean that all of life's problems will go away as we get healthier and develop our relational capacities and talents. *And it definitely does not mean at all that hurting people "cause" their own issues.* Bad things happen to good people, and those bad events affect them. That is not their "fault." For example, oftentimes lonely people have been horribly neglected or abused in life. That is not their fault . . . at all. *God is always on the side of the oppressed.*

But even when we experience life circumstances that were not our fault but that affect our performance in key areas of life, *we have to work on overcoming those injuries and developing our insides.* God heard the cry of the Israelites who were slaves in Egypt, and he rescued them. But they had to go through the journey of getting to the Promised Land through faith and spiritual growth. They had to learn God's "ways" in order to become prosperous (Deuteronomy 6). Likewise, if we have suffered abuse and are afraid to trust people, which would be very normal, we still have to focus on growing in that area so that we can develop relationships with others.

I recently had a great experience coaching a businessman who was held back for many years because of the negative feelings he had about himself and a lack of confidence. Those feelings came directly from his grandfather and father, both of whom were very cruel and demeaning. As a result, he lacked confidence and the ability to experience failure without feeling like he was a loser. He had been stuck at a certain level of performance. He would hit a ceiling and not be able to get past it. How he saw himself inside his own heart limited him, as he still heard the voices of his father and grandfather.

But, through coaching, he developed his *internal* world and got past the limits of his heart. As he did, his "issues" changed. His new issues were more about how to manage and multiply his new successes than about licking his wounds over past failures. Which gets us to the second huge implication:

Spiritual health saves us from going down the wrong path to find a life.

One of the biggest never-go-back learnings occurs when a person realizes that the resolution to their problems does not lie in finding an external solution, like . . .

- I would be happy if I could just move to a big city.

- I would be happy if I could find a mate.

- I would be happy if I could find a better job.

- I would be happy if I could trade in my spouse.

- I would be happy if I made more money.

People who are happy know that their happiness does not depend on external factors, but internal ones. They know that if they are not happy in a small town, they won't be happy in a big one until they resolve whatever inside is making them unhappy. As we've noted before, they know that unhappy single people become unhappy married people. They know that if they have not found their passion and meaning, no future job can "give" it to them. They know that if they cannot be intimate in their current relationship, they would repeat the same pattern in another one. They know that more money will not make them happy and will not fill the emptiness of their life.

> People who are happy know that their happiness does not depend on external factors, but internal ones.

So, they do not give in to fantasy and move somewhere in a search of a "new life." Instead, they get healthy. They make an *internal* life change, not an external one. *They own that even if they move, even if they get rich, even if they get married . . . they will still need to work on their issues.*

Now, it is absolutely true that you might have to move to find a place that has the resources to work on your life or the industry to help you find a job. Or it may be true that having a little more money might enable you to invest in the passion you have discovered. Certainly we live in a relationship with an external world, and the Promised Land truly is better than Egypt! I am not in any way saying that the city where you live or the person you marry or the job you have or your financial situation do not affect life. Of course the outside matters, and I hope you find the best of all those categories.

Here is what I am saying:

> *Successful people—in all of those categories—*
> *know that only as they get healthy will they*
> *thrive and find the external life they desire.*
> *They know that trying to move forward without*
> *aligning the internal life is folly.*

Said another way: "If I hate my life, moving my same life to another building is not going to help." I remember a struggling college fraternity brother saying before Christmas break that he was going to Colorado to find himself. When we all got back in January, we asked him how his trip to find himself went.

He said, "I went to Colorado to find myself, but I wasn't there."

We all cracked up laughing, as did he, but the principle was shouting out:

> *Wherever you go, there you are.*
> *Whatever you own, you are still the same person.*
> *Whoever you are with, you are still you.*
> *Wherever you work, you are still the same person.*

There is a story about a man who moves to a new town to start a new life. He pulls into a gas station where an old man is managing the store. He walks up to the old man and says, "So, I am just moving here. What are the people like around here?"

"What were they like in the last place you lived?" the old man says.

"They were okay, I guess."

The old man looks at him and wisely says, "Well, that's probably how you'll find the people here."

How true. People who see others as good and trustworthy and who establish good relationships tend to do that wherever they go. Those who think the people in their current location are "no good" tend to expect that in their new place "people will be nice." But because they see through the same lens, after a while, the people in the new place don't look nice at all. These people fail to see that their "way of seeing" determines a lot of what they find. Something on the inside makes them see all people as basically untrustworthy, no matter where they are. If you don't believe me, watch a political talk show with a Republican and a Democrat talking about someone in office. They will see the exact same behavior in totally opposite ways—all because of their "inside" bias. One will say, "What an idiot for doing that," and the other will say, "Best president we have had in decades." What we see is often in the eyes of the beholder.

> Our "way of seeing" determines what we find.

It's all on the inside.

Spiritual Qualities Determine Life Outcome

Research affirms what God has told us all along. Possessing spiritual qualities inside and exhibiting the behaviors that emanate from those qualities are what brings personal fulfillment. While this is certainly not an exhaustive list, here are just a few of the internal spiritual qualities that God tells us to develop and that research shows lead to happiness:

- *Love*: "Loving people" are connected people, and connection makes people thrive in all areas of life, from emotions to health to reaching goals.

- *Giving*: People who give of themselves, their talents, and their treasures thrive in a way that those who do not give or serve others don't.

- *Faith*: People with an active spiritual life are healthier and do better on a number of life-satisfaction measures.

- *Activity*: People who are active instead of passive and who take responsibility for creating a life tend to have one.

- *Gratitude*: People who actively develop an attitude of gratitude and express gratitude regularly are happier people.

- *Positive Thinking*: People who guard their thinking and whose thinking is rooted in faith are happier than pessimistic, negative thinkers. They are also more successful.

- *Purpose and Calling*: People who recognize and develop an internal calling and purpose in their lives are more fulfilled.

- *Talents*: People who invest themselves in developing their real talents and strengths and then put them to use are more fulfilled.

- *Humility*: People who are humble enough to receive correction and feedback become wiser and improve over time.

- *Righteousness*: People who develop character that operates in sync with God's "righteousness" and "ways"—such as love, freedom, forgiveness, fruitfulness—thrive.

One night, during dinner with my kids, Lucy brought up something that had happened between her sister, Olivia, and one of her friends—something that activated my radar concerning "what's on the inside." It seems that Olivia had done something to hurt the feelings of a friend of hers, and that friend had told my Lucy about the incident. I asked Olivia what had happened.

"Nothing," she said. "She shouldn't be bugged by it at all. I didn't do anything to hurt her. She just felt left out and is mad at me and not telling me about it. She tells Lucy instead. It's not my fault."

I immediately got scared. Not because of this one instance, but for Olivia's future. One of the downsides to being a psychologist and a parent is that when your kids do something small, like not eating their vegetables, you see a future of prison sentences, failed careers, and twenty-six marriages. You worry that each event will become a character trait that will follow them for life. So I jumped on it.

"That's right," I said. "She should have come to you. But now that you know that her feelings were hurt, what are you going to do about it?"

"Well, nothing. She shouldn't be hurt by it; and if she is, she should say something to me, not tattle to Lucy," she retorted. "Why am I the one in trouble?"

"Livi . . ." I said, "you are not in trouble. Who's at fault is not what is important here. What is important is that you have a friend whose feelings are hurt, and you care about her, right?"

"Of course," she said.

"Well, if you do care about her, and she is hurting, even if you were not in the wrong, what is the thing to do?" I asked.

"Ask her what is wrong and talk to her about it so she feels better," she said.

"Right. So do that, okay?" I said.

"Got it," she said.

Then we went on with dinner. But there is no way I would have ignored that incident—for the very reason of this chapter. Psycho-psychologist father aside, I *know* that Olivia's future external life, the quality of her relationships, and everything else is going to depend on her character and being able to do relationships the "right" way. In this instance, when there is a problem, talk to the person and try to work it out. I did see Olivia's future quality of life flash before my eyes if she became a person who does not lean into conflict and resolve things. So, I helped her to do it.

Think of it this way. If I, as a feeble, limited earthly parent, know enough about my kids' future to help them develop their internal abilities and their character so that they have a good life, doesn't it make sense that God is always telling us that if we'll get our act together, things will go better for us? Having a better life is not always about finding a new friend or job or external solution to our problems. It is first and foremost about making sure that we have the internal character and capacity to *have* a good life if one shows up. He cares about us that much.

> Having a better life is about making sure that we have the internal character and capacity to *have* a good life if one shows up.

Yes, seek great things on the outside. As my father used to say, "Son, money can't buy you happiness, but it *can* buy you a big red Cadillac to go look for it in." If you have your heart set on an external goal like a job or a dream home, I hope you get it! But, make no mistake: It will not make you happy if you are not happy and fulfilled on the inside. Seek God, his kingdom, and his ways first. If you do, the outside will take care of itself.

PART TWO

Now What?

CHAPTER 11

MAKING SURE YOU NEVER GO BACK

Sometimes I want to light my hair on fire when I hear the phrases "She must just not want it bad enough" or "If he really wanted it, he would do it."

Many people think that the most important ingredient in accomplishing goals or change is the desire or motivation to do it. They think that if someone has the desire, they will pull it off. "If you want it bad enough, you can do it," they say. Conversely, if someone does not "do it," then they are guilty of not wanting it bad enough. Not willing to make the sacrifice.

AGGHHH! This drives me crazy for several reasons.

First, this is not what the research shows. In fact, research shows that desire and accomplishment of goals can actually be inversely correlated. In other words, sometimes the more something matters to us, the less apt we are to make it happen. The reason is that if we fail to achieve what we desire because we do not possess the skills, discipline, help, information, and other things necessary to pull it off, then we end up being very depressed and give up altogether. How many people, for example, have you known who truly would like to lose a lot of weight, but have not been able to? As a result, they get depressed and hopeless and quit trying. Sometimes they eat more. The Bible puts it this way, "Hope deferred makes the heart sick, but a longing fulfilled is a tree of life" (Proverbs 13:12, NIV). Our desire can really depress us if we are not able to bring it to fruition.

> Sometimes the more something matters to us, the less apt we are to make it happen.

Second, while desire is important, it is not what enables us to accomplish change. There are many ingredients that make change—and the sustaining of that change—possible; and many of them come from outside ourselves. So when we do not have the ingredients, know-how, and help we need, we are pretty much left to the abilities we already have and the results we were already getting. Knowing that I should never go back, and being *able* not to go back are two entirely different things.

For example, remember the principle *you can't please everyone*? You might now have the knowledge that this is an important life principle, but when you find yourself in a situation that requires you to stand firm against someone you want to please, you begin to feel anxious and weak in the knees. Knowing that this person would be very unhappy if you don't do what he wants you to do—even though you firmly believe that what he wants would not be right for you—you give in at the last moment just to keep him happy. All of your best planning and intentions to stand up for yourself fall flat, and you find yourself in a situation you did not want, resenting the person you wanted to please, and angry at yourself. Discouragement sets in, and you forget your path of change. Back to the old you.

Welcome to the "how to" part of *10 Things I'll Never Do Again*. So far, we have seen ten powerful awakenings, ten patterns of change that can bring you new life. But I don't want you to just read them, make a resolution to change, and then not be able to pull it off. As I said earlier, that can lead to hopelessness, and we don't want that.

This part is about the ingredients, the steps, and the process that is involved when we want to use an awakening to truly change a life-pattern so that we "never go back."

This part is composed of simple concepts and little tips. Some of them will be easy for you, some not so easy. But, remember, if it were easy, you would have already done it—and all of those New Year's resolvers would be skinny, too.

The good news is that God's ways work. Truly. So, let's get to it.

———

CHAPTER 12

WAKE UP!

When you are sleeping, there are a few different ways to wake up:

- You have had enough sleep, and you wake up naturally.

- You read somewhere that getting up and doing something healthy is good for you, so you are motivated to get up.

- Someone else is waking up, and their movement wakes you up.

- Someone wakes you up because they know you have to be somewhere.

- Someone wakes you up because they want you to go somewhere with them.

- Your house is on fire, and you jump out of bed.

- Your child is crying, and you wake up to go help.

- Your alarm goes off, and you get up.

- Your alarm goes off, you think about it for a second, and hit the snooze button for a little more sleep.

"Never going back" is pretty much like waking up, in all its forms. One of the titles I considered for this book (besides "Repent") was "Awakenings." In fact, the Bible refers to it as a "waking-up process." Here is what the book of Ephesians says:

> *Have nothing to do with the fruitless deeds of*
> *darkness, but rather expose them. It is shameful even*
> *to mention what the disobedient do in secret. But*
> *everything exposed by the light becomes visible—*
> *and everything that is illuminated becomes a light.*
> *This is why it is said:* "Wake up, sleeper, rise from the dead,
> and Christ will shine on you."
> *Be very careful, then, how you live—not as unwise but as*
> *wise, making the most of every opportunity, because the*
> *days are evil. Therefore do not be foolish, but understand*
> *what the Lord's will is.*
> *—Ephesians 5:11–17, NIV (emphasis added)*

I love that passage because it describes the process so well. The first part of the process is to realize that what we have been doing is "fruitless." What an awakening! All of the effort and energy we have been spending has not led to what we need and want. It has been *fruitless*. If you review the ten negative patterns we have covered, you'll see that this scripture applies to all of them. They bring no fruit; nothing of value comes from them. In fact, the opposite is true: *they bring pain and destruction*. So, waking up and coming out of denial is the first step in deciding that we want to have "nothing to do with the fruitless deeds of darkness." Back to my favorite word: "repent," meaning to change our mind about what we are doing and to turn in a different direction. Turn around and never go back.

Second, the scripture says these deeds are "shameful." And we *are* ashamed of the patterns that have not brought fruitfulness in our lives.

But then we see that there is hope. The third "step" this scripture describes is getting honest about these patterns and *exposing* them. When we do this, the lights come on. Basically, exposure means to bring something into the light and see it for exactly what it is: fruitless. Worthless. Not bringing any life or value.

When you really look at a pattern and what it has been costing you and shine the light on it, it is exactly like opening up the drapes in the morning or turning on the overhead light: *you wake up.* Why do we wake up? Because, as the passage teaches, time is passing, "the days are evil"—meaning that if we do not wake up, more days are not going to help, and our patterns will continue down the worthless, fruitless path. Nothing gets better on its own. Left alone, these patterns will destroy life. But if we realize that time is running out, and really get that, we will wake up, get out of bed, and get to where we need to go.

> Nothing gets better on its own. Left alone, these patterns will destroy life.

How Do *You* Wake Up?

Now, back to the wake-up call and the various ways it comes. I want you to first recognize how *you* are waking up so you are aware of what is happening in your life. Let's look at the list again:

- *You have had enough sleep, and you wake up naturally.*

  Sometimes you have simply had enough of the way you are living out one of these patterns, and you realize, "I don't want to do this anymore. I want to change." There is no fire alarm, no crisis, no one nagging. Your old ways have just run their course; and like a friend of mine says, "I am too old for this." That response is not measured in years. It is measured by realizing that something's time has passed, and it is time to mature.

- *You read somewhere that getting up and doing something healthy is good for you, so you are motivated to get up.*

  God speaks to us in many, many ways. As Proverbs says, "Out in the open wisdom calls aloud, she raises her voice in the public square (Proverbs 1:20, NIV). And further, "For the LORD gives wisdom; from his mouth come knowledge and understanding (Proverbs 2:6, NIV).

  Heeding wisdom will give us life, but ignoring wisdom will hurt us. There are basically two ways to learn— the easy way and the hard way. The easy way is when someone shares wisdom with us, and we actually listen and follow it. We'll talk more about the hard way later, but suffice it to say, listening to and following wisdom is much better and less costly. In the easy way, we learn the lesson from someone else's mistakes and avoid making the same ones ourselves. Others pay for the mistake, and we get the lessons for free.

Sometimes we read something or hear a sermon or something on the radio, and we instantly recognize it as true—and we follow it. For example, the Surgeon General's Warning concerning lung cancer is worth listening to. Listening is by far the better way to wake up.

• *Someone else is waking up, and their movement wakes you up.*

Another way to "wake up" is to observe someone else doing life in a different way, and we like what we see. Their growth and improved life "nudges" us—like when the person sleeping next to you gets out of bed. You are awakened by the other person's movement, and you get up as well.

• *Someone wakes you up because they know you have to be somewhere.*

Without knowing it, you might be sleeping your life away in a stalled pattern. You may be stuck in your current predicament with no prospects of moving forward. But maybe your friends, family, or advisors are able to see that by staying where you are, you'll never get where you want to get to, so they wake you up and tell you the truth. As Proverbs tells us, the wounds of a friend are better than the kisses of an enemy (see Proverbs 27:6). We're fortunate when we have people in our lives who care enough about us to tell us what they see, even if it's unpleasant—kind of like someone waking us up and telling us that we are late getting somewhere.

- *Someone wakes you up because they want you to go somewhere with them.*

I love this one. It is when someone has discovered something that changes their life and they want you to have it, too. Sometimes one of your friends or mentors learns something about a life-pattern that you are sleeping through, and they want you to have the freedom they have found. Many people share their faith for this very reason; they know what God has done for them and they tell others. When this happens to you—even if your friend seems like a nag—wake up and go with them.

- *Your house is on fire, and you jump out of bed.*

It's hard to sleep through a fire. Some people "get it" only when a crisis of enormous pain forces them awake. Perhaps a heart attack wakes them up from an unhealthy lifestyle. Or a bad relationship becomes abusive. Or maybe they discover a note on their bed that says their spouse has left and is "not able to take it anymore."

Although being awakened by a "fire" is the most painful wake-up call, many lives are changed as a result of a crisis. The main thing to remember is this: if your house is on fire, get up. Period. Do not ignore a crisis. If that particular crisis doesn't wake you up, you will assuredly have another one. Trust me.

- *Your child is crying, and you wake up to go help.*

None of us live in a vacuum. We are connected to others, so our destructive patterns affect them. We inflict "collateral damage." When we live in unwise life-patterns, someone else is usually crying from the pain that those patterns cause. That should get us out of bed.

If one of your patterns is causing loss, pain, or the delay of goodness for someone you care about, chances are that they are crying in some form or fashion. Stop hearing it as criticism that disturbs your sleep, and hear it for what it is: a true cry for help to the only person who can do anything about you: you. Listen for evidence of any pain you are causing, and wake up if someone is crying.

- *Your alarm goes off, and you get up.*

"I dodged a bullet," my friend said. He had almost taken a job with someone, but they ended up hiring someone else. He later found out that the company was corrupt and being sued by multiple parties and was probably headed for bankruptcy. This caused an alarm to go off—a wake-up call. He realized one of these truths we've looked at: He had not done his due diligence. In fact, he often jumped into things too quickly.

We can experience an awakening when we are face-to-face with an "almost train wreck" or an actual one. If this man had taken the job and had gotten pulled into a mess of corruption and lawsuits, he would have most certainly heard an alarm as well. Sometimes, a bad outcome is the best thing that can happen to us when we're living in a bad pattern. It truly wakes us up, and we know that we don't want to do "that" again. We are jolted fully awake and forced to abandon our denial.

Or . . .

- *Your alarm goes off, you think about it for a second, and hit the snooze button for a little more sleep.*

Sometimes wake-up calls happen in an instant, and sometimes it is a process. You might hear the alarm and simply ponder it. In research literature, this is referred to as the "prechange" or "contemplation" stage. You hear the alarm, but you don't get out of bed—not yet. You try to steal a little more sleep, until finally you wake up.

This is where you might be: you're beginning to see that one or more of your life-patterns is costing you, but you're hitting the snooze button—perhaps just contemplating change . . . dreaming about it. But remember, you are not awake until you stop snoozing.

So the first step in never going back is . . .

Wake up.
Any way you can.
Whatever it takes.

Our wake-up process only begins when we fully embrace the *need* to wake up. We may embrace that need for three basic reasons: (1) "I don't want this pain anymore" (we want something negative to stop), or (2) "I want something better than this" (we want something positive to happen), or (3) "I do not want to hurt anyone anymore." All three reasons are good, and they are usually related. But to get our feet out of bed and onto the floor, we must come out of denial and see that the time for snoozing is over. We must be convinced that our current patterns are costing us in pain or missed life. It is time to change.

Play the Movie

One of the best things we can do to help ourselves wake up is what I call "play the movie." Basically, it means that whatever we are doing, we need to see it as one scene in a longer movie and play it out to the end. How does the movie end?

"A moment on the lips, forever on the hips." Playing this movie reveals that the bag of chips or cookies might taste good now, but if I look down the road a bit, I will not like what follows. If I play the scene after this one and after that one, I might see myself fifty pounds heavier. Or having no savings in ten years. Or giving in to someone in five years the same way that I am giving in today. Or, or, or . . .

God has given us the ability to look ahead. It is what psychologists call "hypothetical thinking" and "observing ego." It is the ability to look at our behavior and see where it will get us, then decide whether or not we like what we see. The "law of sowing and reaping" is expressed in Scripture:

> *Do not be deceived:*
> *God cannot be mocked.*
> *A man reaps what he sows.*
> *—Galatians 6:7, NIV*

This is not a spanking. It is a description of how the universe works. God has set up certain laws that the universe obeys. Actions do not exist in a vacuum; they are not events unto themselves. They lead to consequences. We are free to choose our actions, but, unfortunately, we are not free to choose the consequences. They will be what they will be, and we have little control over the consequences; we only control the actions. We sow, and then the reaping comes.

> We are free to choose our actions, but, unfortunately, we are not free to choose the consequences.

God tells us to think about how we are living in the context of not only what it feels like today, but where it leads to tomorrow. *What will the result be if I continue to do what I am doing?* Look down the road and see where it is leading you; play the movie. As the saying goes, "Insanity is doing the same thing expecting different results."

So if you've "played the movie" and are convinced that it does not end well, then you are ready to change. You are awake!

Get Rid of the Guilt

As people begin to wake up to things they need to change, they often get stalled by the two biggest deterrents to change: *guilt* or *shame*. Guilt and shame make you feel that because you have not been able to do it so far, something is wrong with you or you are "bad" in some way. As a result, the focus becomes on how bad you feel instead of on the real problem: What needs to change.

Listen to the words of Jesus:

> *I did not come to judge [condemn] the world,*
> *but to save the world.*
> *—John 12:47, NIV*

His message to you is "Don't feel bad about where you have been or where you are. I want to help you." Remember that Jesus says that there is no condemnation for those who are his. You can be confident of his forgiveness (see Romans 8:1).

So, as you are waking up to the changes you need to make, simply come clean. Admit that what you have been doing is not working and know that it is okay to be where you are. Ask him to forgive you and he will. Once you do that, you are on the doorway to real life change. You are awake!

Where Are You in Waking Up?

So the question becomes, Where are you in the waking-up cycle? Are you dead asleep, totally unaware of the patterns that are keeping you stuck? Are you hitting the snooze button? Are friends and others talking to you, and are you listening?

Research shows that the "wake-up" part of change happens in a path, a process. First we are in the sleeping mode—fumbling around with the idea of change but not getting anywhere; then we rouse a bit, becoming aware of the need for change—usually contemplating it for a while; finally, we get out of bed and take at least one step to implement change. Discovering where you are is very important.

I would like for you to answer the question of where you are in the wake-up process before we move on. How awake are you to a pattern that has been keeping you stuck? What alarms are going off? What pain is speaking to you? Who is talking to you?

Who do you see changing their life in a way that looks good to you? What crisis is telling you that change is needed?

Suggestion: Get a pen and paper; or your phone, tablet, or computer; and get very specific about the questions above. Be honest with yourself about where you are in the wake-up process. Write down the incidents and people that are speaking to you. Write down the consequences that patterns have cost you. In the words of Proverbs, "Give careful thought to the paths for your feet and be steadfast in all your ways" (Proverbs 4:26, NIV).

Continuing to sleep while the alarm is going off is not good. As the Bible says, "Wake up, sleeper." Change is knocking at the door.

CHAPTER 13

THE TRUTH ABOUT SELF-HELP

I was talking to a friend of mine who has gone through amazing changes in the last few years based on the ten principles we have been discussing. When I told her I was writing this book and about real change beginning with a wake-up call—admitting that what we are not doing is not working—she shared her experience with that stage: "What you're saying is absolutely right, but once I really realized that what I was doing was just not working, I found myself in a really dark place. It was hard to admit that I couldn't do it, and when I finally did, it was really dark for a while."

"Tell me more?" I prompted, hoping for the right answer.

"Because even though I knew that what I'd been doing was not working, I didn't know what to do differently or how to do it. That feeling is one of total helplessness—I felt hopeless."

"Yet, here you are," I said. "You got through it, and your life is different now. So what did you do?"

She thought for a moment. "I asked for help," she said. "I

asked God to help me, and I reached out to a few people, and that is when it began. People and answers began to show up."

Right answer. And the key to *everything*:

Self-help is an oxymoron.

The Big Conversion

Want to make a lot of money? Sell people a product that promises to change their lives based on the assertion that they can "do it" if they just decide to. Classic example? Gym memberships in January.

People have made fortunes by building gyms and selling memberships to scores of people who make New Year's resolutions to get in shape around the beginning of the year. The customers "decide" to get in shape and lose weight, pay the fees, and sign up for a year or more. They are ready, filled with "desire."

They begin well, and then about the third or fourth week, they slowly stop going. By the spring, they have all but forgotten their membership at the club and the workouts have stopped.

Who wins? The people who own the club, which is being paid for largely by the people who never use it. The owners never have to clean up after them, service them, buy new equipment that they wore out, hire new staff to help them, or do anything else for people who never show up—other than send them a monthly bill. Pretty good business model. Sell services to people who don't cash in on what they have paid for.

Why does this formula work? *Because of our incurable belief that we can do things just because we "desire" them.* We think, "I want to do that" or "reach that goal," and then we launch on a plan to pull it off. But oftentimes, once we start, we run out of steam, motivation, or ability, and we give up. We hit obstacles, get confused and discouraged, and so we fail. Or maybe we just get busy with other things that we "have to do." For whatever reason, our best intentions go by the wayside. And we "go back." We do what we were doing before—and we go through this cycle again and again.

> The "big conversion" is realizing that we cannot do it on our own.

So, the "big conversion" is realizing that we cannot do it on our own. We need help from outside ourselves.

There's No Such Thing as Self-Help

One of the most important truths we will ever learn in life is that there is no such thing as "self-help." Physics teaches us that a "closed system" runs down over time. It runs out of energy, and it hits the limit of its own "know-how." Einstein said it best: "We cannot solve our problems with the same thinking we used when we created them."

I'm not trying to say that we cannot do things for ourselves or that we can't make changes. Self-improvement and growth and maturing are important and valid aspects of the successful life. The last thing we want is to be totally unable to make changes or do things for ourselves.

But there are times when we truly *can't* do something ourselves. If a car is out of gas, it cannot "self-gas." It must get gas from outside itself. It does not have extra gas on the inside.

In order for a plant to grow, it needs minerals, air, water, and sunlight. It needs to be fertilized and fed from outside itself. It cannot "self-help" its way to maturity. If your body is to grow new cells and capacities, it needs vitamins, minerals, fuel, and the like in order to do its "self-improvement." It has to take in from the outside what it does not possess already. It can't just "grow it." At those times, we need help.

So if you already possess the ability to change your behavior and thinking simply by learning the ten principles and understanding them, that is awesome. Sometimes we are able to learn new insights, gain new knowledge and wisdom, and then put what we've learned into practice. Sometimes we are able to change our ways and become stronger. Go for it if you are able!! Do it!

For example, if you read the principle about doing due diligence and you suddenly had a flash of insight, saying, "That is me! That's why I have gotten into the last five messes of my life. I jump too quickly and do not see the downsides." Then you are able—just through learning—to exercise that wisdom and utilize self-control the next time and be patient—not instantly falling in love with something or someone and jumping too soon. Great.

But chances are that in some areas, you are not able to just read it and do it—like the people who make a New Year's resolution to get in shape. They resolve to do it, but do not possess the lasting motivation or the discipline to keep it going. If they rely only on desire, understanding and commitment, they will fall short when their old patterns kick in and their best-laid plans will be sabotaged. If they remain a "closed system"—thinking they can change themselves without any help from the outside— they will not succeed.

I chuckled recently as I read a book by a researcher who argued that people can change on their own. He contended that you can "change yourself" without therapy or other professional help or a program or help of any kind. "You can do it all yourself," he said. "Just follow this program."

Then the "self-help" program proceeded to suggest joining support systems, groups, and buddy systems; getting accountability partners; gaining knowledge, etc. Joining those "help" systems is exactly the opposite of "self-help," although continuing to call it self-help sounds good and sells books.

Of course not everyone needs professional therapy to change her life. But I do believe that everyone needs help from outside themselves, and research backs that up. Professional or nonprofessional—we need each other.

So, after you wake up and come out of denial, your first action step is to admit that you cannot do it on your own and that you need to reach outside yourself to get from others what you don't have on your own.

This is the heart of the Bible's message: We need help from two power sources larger than just ourselves: God and other people.

Our Powerlessness versus God's Power and Help

A few decades ago, the recovery movement (the 12 Step Program) began to get popular in churches. That was a good thing. The entire tradition begins with a step that says "we admit that we are powerless . . ." over whatever the addiction happens to be. It is basically waving the white flag, saying, "I give up. Everything I have tried is not working. I can't fix this."

But some preachers and religious folks did not like the message that recovery begins with our stating that we are "powerless."

I remember a debate with a rigid pastor who said, "Being 'powerless' is a cop-out! People are not powerless; we are free moral agents, and everyone is responsible for their actions. You cannot claim the excuse of powerlessness."

This sounds so "responsible," right? It sounds so right to tell people to take responsibility for their addictions or other patterns, instead of allowing them to cop out and play the "disease" or "inability" card. "Just stop using drugs!" they say. "You are responsible for yourself." Here is what I said to him:

"That sounds so morally right, so superior, and like such a strong message," I began. "Telling people that they are not powerless but responsible sounds 'God-fearing and righteous.' But the truth is that the Bible's message is way, way, way tougher than yours. It is a *lot* tougher."

"What do you mean?" he said. "How can you be tougher than telling people to be responsible for their lives?"

"I'll tell you how. And it is exactly what the Bible *and* the reality of life tell us every day:

> *You truly are powerless to change yourself.*
> *You truly are unable.*
> *AND . . . you are responsible for yourself.*

"So how does *that* message feel? When you put *inability* and *responsibility* together, you really are painted into a corner. You are now responsible for your life, *and* you are unable to do anything about it. That is a much tougher message," I said. "And it only leads to one place: '*Please, somebody help me.*' "

That is the Bible's core message: we truly do need help, *and* we are unable to help ourselves. But the message does not stop there. It goes on to offer the ultimate hope: the God who created you desires to come into your life and help you "never go back." The infinite source of power and wisdom says that he will invade all your life-patterns and help you change them. He will lead you to the answers and provide the abilities that you do not have. *All you have to do is ask.*

> We truly do need help, *and* we are unable to help ourselves. But the message does not stop there.

This is the ultimate answer to how my friend got out of the "really dark place" that she described when facing the truth. She realized that she could not do it herself, and she began to cry out to God for help. And he began to give it. She found that what Jesus said was true:

"Come to Me, all of you who are weary and burdened,
and I will give you rest.
All of you, take up My yoke and learn from Me,
because I am gentle and humble in heart,
and you will find rest for yourselves.
For My yoke is easy and My burden is light."
—Matthew 11:28–30, HCSB

The first step in doing what we have never been able to do before is to not continue to try on our own, but to ask for God's help. He promises that he will help us, and he truly does—in several ways:

1. He Gives Us Strength to Do What We Cannot Do on Our Own Strength

Fear not, for I am with you;
be not dismayed, for I am your God;
I will strengthen you, I will help you,
I will uphold you with my righteous right hand.
—Isaiah 41:10, NIV

Have you not known? Have you not heard?
The LORD is the everlasting God, the Creator of the
ends of the earth.
He does not faint or grow weary; his understanding
is unsearchable.
He gives power to the faint,

and to him who has no might he increases strength.
Even youths shall faint and be weary,
and young men shall fall exhausted;
but they who wait for the Lord shall renew their strength;
they shall mount up with wings like eagles;
they shall run and not be weary; they shall walk and not faint.
—Isaiah 40:28–31, ESV

I cannot tell you how many times I have heard people who are making difficult changes say something like, "I don't know how to explain it other than God gave me strength." In the moments when you feel like you "might go back," reach out to God and say, "God, I need your strength to do this." He will provide it.

2. He Leads Us into the Truth We Need in Order to Resolve the Issues We Are Dealing With

I will instruct you and teach you in the way you should go;
I will counsel you with my eye upon you.
—Psalm 32:8, ESV

Send out your light and your truth; let them lead me;
let them bring me to your holy hill and to your dwelling!
—Psalm 43:3, ESV

As you are going forward and putting these awakenings into practice, actively ask God to show you what you need to know.

Ask him to speak to you and to send you the insights, wisdom, truths, and learning that will make it all work. I love his promise

_____

Rather than
pointing the
finger, shaming or
condemning, God
reaches out to help.

_____

in the book of James that we looked at before, where he says that he will generously give wisdom "without finding fault!" He does not get on our case when we get it wrong and screw up over and over. He does not "find fault" in our failures and lack of completeness. The opposite is true: rather than pointing the finger, shaming or condemning, he reaches out to help.

3. He Guides Our Path and Orders Our Steps

God will bring us the experiences, people, and circumstances we need, and he will lead us to where we need to be.

> *Commit your way to the LORD;*
> *trust in Him, and He will act.*
> —Psalm 37:5, HCSB

> *And I will lead the blind in a way that they*
> *do not know,*
> *in paths that they have not known I will guide them.*
> *I will turn the darkness before them into light,*
> *the rough places into level ground.*
> *These are the things I do, and I do not forsake them.*
> —Isaiah 42:16, ESV

Trust in the LORD with all your heart,
and do not lean on your own understanding.
In all your ways acknowledge him,
and he will make straight your paths.
—Proverbs 3:5,6, ESV

Everyone I know who makes significant never-go-back changes has a story of how the "next steps" in their path revealed themselves one after another. The common theme in their stories is that they could not always see the next step, and for sure could not see the one after that; but as they got moving, the steps would appear.

That is how God usually works. Most of the time, he does not give us the whole plan, the whole map, or even the end point. He just leads us, opening and closing doors as we go along, directing our paths to where we need to go. As we saw earlier in Proverbs 16:9, "In their hearts humans plan their course, but the LORD establishes their steps" (NIV). He will get us where we need to go, as we trust him; he will lead us to a place where we will never go back to old, dead-end ways.

4. He Brings Us Strength and Other Help Through Other People

Research shows over and over again that the change-process happens best and most successfully with the help of other people. There are all sorts of scientific reasons for this, from the way the brain works to our biochemistry, but the bottom line is that what we get from other people is essential to change.

Eight Readily Available Ingredients for Change

Following are eight essential ingredients for change that we get from other people and from God. They are there for your taking—you just have to reach out and ask:

1. *Support:* People who support us in making changes give us strength, lending us the encouragement and energy we need to continue when it gets hard.

2. *Connection:* Making changes sometimes causes us to take difficult stands that threaten some relationships. We need other connections so we are not alone in the conflict.

3. *Discipline:* Change involves building new muscles that we did not have before, and that always takes discipline. Sometimes "self-discipline" wanes as things get tough; and we need others to keep us on track. We need to be disciplined by and through them.

4. *Accountability:* When we are accountable to others to follow through on our commitments, our success rate goes up.

5. *Forgiveness:* Change is usually two steps forward, one back. One of the biggest obstacles to change is the feelings of guilt and discouragement people feel when they fail. The acceptance and forgiveness of others helps us to accept and forgive ourselves and learn from the mistakes we make.

6. *Models and Mentors:* It is difficult for us to do what we have not seen done. We need people to model new things for us and to show us how to do them. A strong relationship with a few models and mentors makes all the difference.

7. *Correction:* As much as we hate it, we need to be confronted and corrected at times in the process of change. Words that are hard to hear are sometimes exactly what we need. As Proverbs says, "Wounds from a friend can be trusted" (27:6, NIV).

8. *Traveling Companions:* Research shows that change is "contagious." Change happens in a strong way when we stay close to others who are making the same changes and accomplishing what we want to accomplish. That is why support networks of people working on similar things are so successful. Research shows this over and over. It normalizes the struggle, we learn from and support each other, and we actually "rub off" on each other, as we influence each other to grow and keep going.

Reversing Physics

As I said before, physics teaches us that a closed system runs down and gets sicker over time. Leave your young kids at home alone for a weekend and see if the house is neater when you return. Left unto themselves, not a big chance.

But any system can be reversed by becoming an "open system" and taking in from the outside what is needed for the changes required. Just like your computer opens its system to the network to download software updates, when we open ourselves to others, we download the updates we need for our own programming.

Just as physics teaches us, when we open the closed system, we open ourselves up to the two big ingredients from God and others that we need:

1. New energy sources
2. New templates in the form of structure, information, or intelligence

To make sure you "never go back" to old ways that don't work, do not remain a closed system unto yourself. Review the previously listed eight "readily available ingredients for change." Look to God and others for the new energy and information you need. When you do, you are doing exactly what the Bible says to do and exactly what scientific research has proven to work.

CHAPTER 14

POWERFUL PRINCIPLES TO MAKE CHANGE HAPPEN

Do you believe in the possibility of life change?

What has your experience with change been?

Have you ever changed a significant area in your life?

Have you found that some life-patterns are very resistant to change?

Do you have hope, or are you discouraged about the possibilities?

All of these are relevant questions. As a fellow traveler in the lifelong process of change, and as one who has walked the path of change with many people over the years, I can relate to all of the above.

In this final chapter, I want to share some simple but very powerful principles on how to make the change you desire a reality. Some of this we have discussed, and some we haven't, but we usually need to be *reminded* more than we need to be *taught*. The reason?

Change is a process.

There is an old story in recovery circles that goes something like this:

My Life in Five Short Chapters

Chapter One: *I went out for a walk, and I fell into a deep, dark hole. It took me a long time to get out.*

Chapter Two: *I went out for a walk, and I fell into the same deep, dark hole. It took me a long time to get out.*

Chapter Three: *I went out for a walk, and I came across the same deep, dark hole. I walked up to it slowly, got very close to it, looked inside the hole . . . and I fell in again. It took me a long time to get out.*

Chapter Four: *I went out for a walk, and I came across the same deep, dark hole. This time as I approached it, I decided to not get too close, and I walked around it.*

Chapter Five: *I went out for a walk.* This time I went down a different street.

So true. Sometimes it takes a while for us to "get it." We are on autopilot, and we repeat patterns in our lives without even knowing that our pattern is what is creating our problems. We just know that we are in a hole and that it takes us a long time to get out. I often say, "We don't need new ways to fail. The old ones are working just fine." It is our patterns that do us in.

But, change happens. Life experience and research will back that up. Even resistant, very difficult patterns can be changed, and the twelve principles below will help you make change a reality.

1. Strive for Progress Not Perfection

Research shows that change happens more consistently and lasts longer when our goal is to get better, not perfect. Changing the ten never-go-back patterns we've spent most of the book talking about is a *process*; and it is going to take some work.

> We repeat patterns in our lives without even knowing that our pattern is what is creating our problems.

When we understand that change is a process, then when we do fall short, we will see it as a necessary part of the path and not as a dead end. We'll be able to take a setback in stride and continue going forward. So remember . . .

We are not aiming for perfection, just progress.

God's story is full of imperfect people who reached the goal—not because they did not make mistakes, but because they remained faithful in a direction.

2. Be Honest with Yourself

Remember the "wake-up call" we talked about earlier? When you hear that call, do not hit "snooze." The first step in making real change is to come out of denial and acknowledge reality for what it is. Being in denial does not mean that you are bad; it just means that you have not been aware of the truth of something. As relates to the ten "awakenings" we've been talking about, until you read this book, you may not have been aware of harmful patterns in your life or their real consequences. You may not have known that going down that street and getting close to the deep, dark hole is doing you in. And if you're actually *in* that hole, maybe you've been unaware of what being there is costing you.

> Being in denial does not mean that you are bad; it just means that you have not been aware of the truth of something.

Now is the time to get honest with yourself. Brutally honest. Now is the time to own what these destructive patterns are doing to your life. You're already *living* the reality of the hole anyway, so you may as well own up to it.

A word of caution here: Don't feel guilty or let shame keep you from admitting what you need to see. Don't feel bad. God forgives you and wants to help, but he can only help us if we agree that there is a problem and own what it is.

3. Realize You Are Not the Entire Solution

In chapter 13 we saw that self-help is an oxymoron. Now of course there are times when we just need someone—maybe me—to point out the problem, and then we are able to turn things around and make the change quickly. So if you're able to do that, by all means "do it!" Even then, we're drawing on the strength that God and others have already helped impart to our lives and can continue to impart in the present moment as well.

But, if there is one or more of these patterns that you cannot change, stop trying to do it on your own, reach outside yourself, and put a never-go-back team together. It might be a support group, therapist, buddy, peer group, mentor, a formal program, or something else. Oftentimes, change can only be empowered by outside sources: God and other people. So reach out and ask for help.

4. See Today's Actions in a Different Time Zone

I like the phrase "play the movie" when trying to get people to take ownership of a pattern in their life (see my book *9 Things You Simply Must Do*). It means to look at what you are doing today and play it forward down the timeline—to see it in a future time zone. It helps you see this current behavior as a scene in a larger movie, your life, and where your life will end up if you continue down this path.

For example, if you are caught up in trying to make people happy, see yourself in a year, two years, or five years down the road. Where will you be? Do you like what you see? You can change your future by changing your current life-patterns. Read on.

5. Believe and Have Vision

Research shows that change happens when we (1) believe that it is possible and (2) have a clear vision of where we want to be. This is another way to think about what the Bible calls faith.

The Bible says that "faith is confidence in what we hope for and assurance about what we do not see" (Hebrews 11:1, NIV). God loves it and is pleased with you when you believe that he can help you do something you think is impossible. It shows that you trust him, and trusting him for what you cannot yet see is always how we get past our limitations.

Think of yourself as the person God is going to help you become. He promises that he will continue to get you there: "I am confident of this, that he who started a good work in you will carry it on to completion until the day of Christ Jesus" (Philippians 1:6, HCSB). Exercise faith and believe that he can help you turn into that person as you follow him. See yourself as someone who is able to turn from the ten practices you have been reading about and develop a new way of doing things:

- Refusing to return to things that have not worked unless there is a good reason

- Never agreeing to be someone you are not

- Determining not to try to change another person into someone they are refusing to be

- Understanding that you cannot please everyone

- Being willing to go through a little pain in the short-term to get something good in the long-term

- Trusting real and authentic people instead of those who try to appear better than they are

- Carefully reviewing the big picture before acting

- Proceeding with prudence and not impulsively jumping into things

- Honestly looking at yourself to see what part you might be playing in every situation

> God loves it and is pleased with you when you believe that he can help you do something you think is impossible.

- Focusing on developing your inside life in order to produce the outside life you desire

See yourself clearly as you and God want you to become. Keep the end in mind, as the Bible often reminds us to do:

Not that I have already obtained all this,
or have already arrived at my goal,
but I press on to take hold of that
for which Christ Jesus took hold of me.
Brothers and sisters, I do not consider myself
yet to have taken hold of it.
But one thing I do: Forgetting what is behind
and straining toward what is ahead,
I press on toward the goal to win the prize
for which God has called me heavenward in Christ Jesus.
—Philippians 3:12–14, NIV

6. Utilize External Gauges and Limits

By definition, you are creating new patterns when you make these changes. What that means is that your brain is currently wired to do it the old way and will default to doing it the old way until new patterns are wired.

One of the important aspects of establishing new patterns is to observe where we are, to monitor ourselves, to measure our progress, and to know our limits. Ideally, this is done in relationship with others who can hold us accountable to how we are doing. Get a buddy or put together a group of others who will hold you accountable to the things you promise yourself to change. The Bible tells us to "admonish one another" (Colossians 3:16) and to "spur one another to love and good deeds" (Hebrews 10:24).

The things we track and monitor get better compared to the things we don't pay attention to. When we focus our attention on our life-patterns and maintain regular accountability, the brain is better able to wire its internal patterns. And pretty soon, those new patterns become part of who we are. But it all begins on the outside. Your brain needs to be made aware of the "gap" and held accountable for where you are in the path in order to advance.

> Pretty soon, those new patterns become part of who we are.

7. Set Up Reminders

Research has shown that when we set up triggers or cues to remind us to do certain behaviors, we are more likely to do them.

In fact, this is something that God told us way before scientists began to find out that it worked:

> *Hear, O Israel: The LORD our God, the LORD is one. Love the LORD your God with all your heart and with all your soul and with all your strength. These commandments that I give you today are to be on your hearts. Impress them on your children. Talk about them when you sit at home and when you walk along the road, when you lie down and when you get up. Tie them as symbols on your hands and bind them on your foreheads. Write them on the doorframes of your houses and on your gates.*
> *—Deuteronomy 6:4–9, NIV*

We know that the brain uses reminders to retrain our behavior. After many repetitions, our patterns become automatic. But without reminders, when there are no patterns, we just go back to our established ways. That is why God tells us over and over throughout the Bible to remind ourselves of what is important so it can become part of us. In the above passage, God told his people to place physical reminders on their bodies as well as their houses and gates.

If you are trying to remember to follow through on these new patterns, remind yourself. Use yellow sticky notes, reminders on your smartphone or computer, three-by-five cards on your fridge, desk, or mirror. Do whatever it takes to make your brain attend to the new things you are trying to get it to do—remind yourself to remind yourself. What if there were a yellow sticky

note on your computer screen that said, "Make the right decision, not the one that is going to make everyone happy"? That
would cause you to stop and think during those critical moments
when the invitation to "go back" arrives in your in-box!

8. Stay Online with God for System Updates

One of the most important teachings of the Bible and realities
of our lives is that we were designed to be connected to God and
his power. And through God's power, he supplies the ability to
live life with a power, truth, and strength that we do not possess
on our own. To truly be all that we were designed to be and
accomplish all that we are able to accomplish, we need to be
plugged in to God and his power. Jesus said it like this:

Remain in Me, and I in you.
Just as a branch is unable to produce fruit by itself
unless it remains on the vine,
so neither can you unless you remain in Me.
I am the vine; you are the branches.
The one who remains in Me and I in him
produces much fruit, because you can do nothing without Me.
If anyone does not remain in Me,
he is thrown aside like a branch and he withers.
—John 15:4–6, HCSB

In some ways, people are a little like computers. *First*, we
sometimes live in ways we were not designed to live—like if you

used a computer to do things it is not programmed to do. It just does not work well. Time to begin acting like a human.

Second, we try to live a full life without being plugged into a power outlet. Computers don't work well without that outside

> Time to begin acting like a human.

energy, and neither do we. We are designed to be "connected" to God and have his life flow through us. Many people realize that they need a "spiritual" dimension, but they aren't really plugged in to the real source.

Third—and this is where the rubber meets the road in being truly fruitful:

Fruitful computers are always "online."

Computers do their work as they are programmed to do, and they do it well. Fine, except for one thing.

It doesn't take long before that computer hits an obstacle that requires new information. Or maybe the computer is unable to do a needed task until it gets a software update or an app is downloaded. Until that happens, it's stuck. But if the computer is online and connected to the Internet, the servers send software updates and fixes that are needed for optimum performance.

We are exactly like that. We need to be "online with God" all the time, every moment. Do not unplug even for a day. Stay in constant relationship with him, as Jesus said above, and "remain in Me." Then, as you encounter obstacles in the day or in relationships or in work, you are constantly asking God to show you what to do and to give you the ability to take the next step. He will download to you what you need. That is way better than living on your own.

9. Fire the Bad Boss Inside

If you have ever heard the term "self-talk," you know what this means. We actually have "voices" in our heads, designed to be there by God. And they guide us. They help us grow, learn, and mature.

When children are small, their parents fill their heads with messages like, "You can do it, just stick to it." "You are loved, even when you fail." "You have gifts and abilities—go use them." "Don't go in the street before you look to your right and left." On and on, these messages are implanted into our heads and become part of our thinking, behaving, and being. It is so automatic that after a point, we do not even know we are thinking them. We just live them out.

But sometimes we get messages from parents or others that are not helpful, but they still dictate our behavior. It's like we have a bad boss in our heads saying, "You're not able to do it. You won't amount to anything." "Who do you think you are, thinking you can do that?" "You're stupid." Etc. etc. Then, because of the way the brain is designed, those messages are internalized as well, and they become part of us, so much so that they can drive the automatic patterns that we have been discussing. We think certain things and do not even know we are thinking them. But we obey them nevertheless.

This is why psychologists emphasize the importance of

healthy self-talk. What research shows is that your internal self-talk is, for the most part, on "automatic"—you are not even aware of the messages that guide you. But when you do become aware of them and change the way you talk to and guide yourself, you change as a person. The Bible says over and over that we are as we think in our hearts (see Proverbs 23:7, NASB) and that we need to "renew our minds" (Romans 12:2). It tells us to "take every thought captive" (2 Corinthians 10:5), as if our thoughts are invaders into the land of our hearts and minds. "Capture the trespassers in your head! Kick them out!" God says.

So, remember two things. First, the voices got there from real voices and came from real experiences. Do not be a closed system, allowing the old tapes—the bad boss—to guide you, but open up and expose yourself to some new voices that support you and believe in you.

But second—and this is key—monitor which voices are playing in your head. Research shows that when you begin to be aware of the negative thinking and the old patterns playing in your head and then counter them with new voices, *you will change*. But to do this, you cannot continue to live on autopilot. You have to become aware of what you are thinking, even writing it down if you need to. Then write down a scripture or an encouraging message from your change team or another loved one and actively begin to substitute those old thoughts with new ones. At first, you will have to con-

> When you begin to be aware of the negative thinking and the old patterns playing in your head and then counter them with new voices, *you will change*.

sciously make the switch—every time—but soon these new, better thoughts will become your autopilot. It truly works, as your head is designed to work that way. Change from "it will be terrible if Joey gets mad at me for making this decision," to "You can't keep everyone happy. If he does not like it, he will have to get over it. And in the meantime, God and my other supporters are with me."

10. Do It Before You Know How

Trying to do something before you actually know how might reek of inauthenticity. I do not like people who fake it, nor, as a psychologist, do I like for people to be told to deny how they feel or what is really going on with them. Putting on a mask will never help us—until we realize that . . .

Faking it is a growth step.

What?? You just said you don't like faking it and then you say it is a growth step? What does that mean? I know. Sorry. Here is what I mean: In order to learn something new or do something different, we have to take a step on the outside before we feel it on the inside. We have to jump out of the plane, even though we are scared to death and do not feel as confident as a Navy SEAL. But, after a lot of jumps, we learn to like skydiving.

Right now, today, you may not feel confident to do some of the things that the ten awakening principles ask you do to, and understandably so. But, here is the truth:

You will never feel confident in doing something
until you have done it.

We have to take a step that we do not feel like taking in order to become confident. Then do it again. We have to do it before we actually know how. That's just the way it is. But that is different from being inauthentic or in denial, which is true "faking it." This good kind of faking it means that we do things in faith before they are part of us, and in taking that step of faith, God brings them to fruition. That is one reason he says: *"In the same way faith, if it doesn't have works, is dead by itself."*

Here is what the book of James says:

But someone will say, "You have faith, and I have works."
Show me your faith without works, and I will show
you faith from my works. You believe that God is one;
you do well. The demons also believe—and they shudder.
Foolish man! Are you willing to learn that
faith without works is useless?
Wasn't Abraham our father justified by works
when he offered Isaac his son on the altar?
You see that faith was active together with
his works, and by works, faith was perfected.
So the Scripture was fulfilled that says,
Abraham believed God, and it was credited to him
for righteousness, and he was called God's friend.
—James 2:17–23, HCSB

So, in this way, because we believe in God and his ways, we take a step of faith to do things his way, convinced that he will help us to become the person we are beginning to act like we are. As the scripture above says about Abraham, "Faith was active together with his works, and by works, faith was perfected." When you have faith that a principle of God's is right and you act on it out of faith, it will become a part of you. And soon, you will feel comfortable with this new way of thinking and acting, no longer afraid.

Begin to live out the principles, even when it is uncomfortable or difficult. That is the only way we grow. But do not be in denial about how you really feel. Acknowledge your true feelings. You cannot talk your brain out of how it feels; in fact, that is counterproductive. Instead of trying to talk yourself out of it, say, "I acknowledge that I am afraid, and this is not going to feel good. But I will ignore my fear and act on what is right anyway." Then run to God and your team and get the support to stay steadfast. It will work. As my eleven-year-old daughter, Lucy, says, "Dad, you have to feel it, ignore it, and then act!" Yay Lucy!

11. Fill the Vacuum

You have heard the statement that nature abhors a vacuum. It will move quickly to fill it up. The same is true about you and your heart and soul. All of the patterns we have discussed come out of a need, such as fear, loneliness, or lack of self-control or wisdom. A lack of love, maturity, support or other such factors can drive us to behaviors such as people-pleasing, trying to become someone we are not, making impulsive choices, etc.

If our hearts are not full of love, sometimes we will make destructive choices in order to fill the hole inside. If our minds are not full of wisdom, we will make naïve and unwise choices. If our souls are not full of strong passion, skills, and identity, we flounder. To stop doing the hurtful ways, we need to get filled up with good things. That is why God's system of change is different from any other—it is designed to be built upon strength not emptiness.

Being required to do things that you are unable to do is a bit like being required to run a race when you have a broken ankle. God wants to fill you up with his love, the love of others, wisdom, skills, and strength so you can live the life and be the person he intended. The Bible tells us that "we love because he first loved us" (1 John 4:19, NIV). When we become aware of God's love for us, we are able to direct that love outward to others. He also tells us, "strengthen your feeble arms and weak knees. 'Make level paths for your feet,' so that the lame may not be disabled, but rather healed" (Hebrews 12:12–13, NIV). He is not asking you to run a race on a broken leg.

When your heart is lonely and needs love and approval, you have a difficult time saying no to someone who is trying to control you or make you become someone you are not. Your unmet needs for approval will overtake your ability to say no.

First, you have to fill your vacuum by strengthening "your feeble arms and weak knees" with the love and strength of God and others. That way, you will not be working from a vacuum when you try to deal with the difficulties that growth demands. God's system is an "overflow" system. He gives you the strength you will need and then asks you to use it. You can't love from an empty heart. Receive his love and the love of others, and then you will be able to give it away.

12. Do the Right Thing, at the Right Time, for the Right Amount of Time

I love this passage from the Psalms:

> *Blessed is the one who does not walk in step with the wicked*
> *or stand in the way that sinners take*
> *or sit in the company of mockers,*
> *but whose delight is in the law of the LORD,*
> *and who meditates on his law day and night.*
> *That person is like a tree planted by streams of water,*
> *which yields its fruit in season and whose leaf does not wither*
> *—whatever they do prospers.*
> *—Psalm 1:1–3, NIV*

God understands that we need to grow before we can produce fruit.

Listen to that phrase: "which yields its fruit in season." In other words, God knows that it is a process to get there. In the same way that he would not expect a tree to sprout an apple on the day it is planted, he understands that we, too, need to grow before we can produce fruit. And successful people understand this truth as well. They realize that time is part of the formula.

But time is not all that's needed. Seasons and continuing to do the right activities of those seasons are part of the process, too. Planting, nurturing, watering, protecting, healing, pruning, weeding, etc., take months and months, and then . . . yes, the harvest. The yield of fruit comes in season—the harvest season that follows all the growth.

My hope for you is that this book will be one more step in God's journey for you and your life, and that, as you put these truths to work, your seasons of cultivating growth will yield the "peaceful fruit of righteousness" (Hebrews 12:11, ESV) and that life will be headed down a different and better road.

To contact Dr. Henry Cloud, please visit him online:

http://www.facebook.com/DrHenryCloud
https://twitter.com/DrHenryCloud

For speaking engagements or other inquiries, email him at info@drcloud.com. For audio and video coaching products, please visit www.drcloud.com.